ADHD BEHIND CLOSED DOORS

Truth Unveiled - Navigating Life With A Child With ADHD Through A Mother's Eyes

MIRKA FROMMENWILER

TABLE OF CONTENTS

ACKNOWLEDGEMENT V

AUTHOR'S NOTE VII

HOW DID I GET HERE? IX

PROLOGUE 1

PART 1
BECAUSE THE EASY WAY IS OVERRATED 3
   Be Careful What You Wish For 3
   Fairy Tale Turned Nightmare 8
   Lost in Mom Translation 15

PART 2
NAVIGATING THE WILD TERRAIN AND
THE BATTLE OF WILLS 19
   He Will Grow Out Of It 19
   Boredom Meets Education 21
   Fleeting Victories 26
   The Principal's Frequent Flyer Program 30
   A Mom's Serenade 38

PART 3
ORDINARY IS OVERRATED 49
In Pursuit of Answers 49
Proudly Perplexed 57
Magic Pill? 62
Short-Lived Therapy 68
Dispatching the Parent Police 70
Shadows of Suffering 74
School Dropout Manifesto 80

PART 4
PUTTING THE PUZZLE TOGETHER 91
Taking the Reins 91
Uniquely Wired Brain 93
Epiphany: Cracking the Code 96
Unlocking My Child's Superpowers 124
Unconventional Education 127
Making the World Work For Your Child 130

ACKNOWLEDGEMENT

I would like to acknowledge all the people who played a part in shaping my story. My gratitude goes out to all the parents I met in parent and family support groups and to everyone who I encountered during my training. Thank you for being so vulnerable, for sharing your life stories with me. Thank you for contributing to my understanding of ADHD and to my growth as a parent.

I am forever grateful to my husband, Tom, for always being there for me and not only supporting me as a parent but also as a writer. A special thank you goes to my best friend—you know who you are! She has been there for me every step of this journey. She was there through the tears and the laughter. She always picked up the phone when I needed to talk to someone and always showed up at my house to support me, even when I said I was 'fine'. I don't think I would have been able to get through all of this without you! I am so lucky to have you in my life.

AUTHOR'S NOTE

I never intended to write a book. This started out as entries in my journal. However, as I was reviewing some of my most recent notes, I realized that reading about my experiences could help other parents who sometimes struggle with aspects of parenthood like I did. Everyone has a story, and this is mine. It is not a story about ADHD. It is the story of my journey as a mother, navigating the labyrinth of my inner thoughts and emotions while doing everything in my power to support my child as he learned to live and thrive with ADHD.

There are parts of this book where my notes were insufficient and I had to rely solely on my memory. I also changed the names of all the characters and identifying characteristics of all professionals to protect their privacy. But the story is true.

HOW DID I GET HERE?

"Who could it be at this hour? It is well past 10," I asked my husband, my heart racing in sync with the gloomy toll of the doorbell.

I opened the door and a pair of policemen emerged from the shadows. "We were called here because of a domestic dispute."

My jaw dropped in disbelief. "What domestic dispute?" I asked, looking very confused.

"May we come in?" one of the officers asked.

Reluctantly, I invited them inside and showed them to our living room.

As they walked in, my husband jumped out of his seat, "What is going on?" he asked.

"We have received a phone call from Jack concerning the confiscation of his phone. He appeared deeply distressed, so we were compelled to investigate and ensure that everything is ok here," one of the officers explained.

"Jack called you?" I stammered, not knowing what else to say.

I took a deep breath and explained, "Jack is our 14-year-old son. We took his phone away as a consequence of his actions."

"May we speak with Jack?" the officer asked firmly. I stood there feeling embarrassed, wishing for the earth to swallow me up. Then I heard my husband calling for Jack. "Jack, can you please come down, there are two police officers here that would like to talk to you."

Jack walked into the living room, his head held high, his shoulders back, looking very proud of himself. He assumed that we would be the ones reprimanded.

To his surprise, things turned out quite differently. The officers took the time to talk to him, explaining that we, as his parents, are the authority figures in the house and we are the ones who make and reinforce the rules.

Jack just stood there, not saying a word. It was obviously not how he envisioned the conversation going.

I apologized to the police officers for the inconvenience caused and showed them to the door. But Jack recovered from this setback almost immediately. As soon as the door was closed, he began asking for his phone, which escalated into a tantrum of great intensity.

As his tantrum echoed through the halls, I braced myself for the unpredictable chapters awaiting us. Chapters that would test the boundaries of parenthood and challenge the very core of our family dynamics. Little did I know that the pages yet to be turned held secrets that would unravel the fabric of our reality, leaving me questioning, "How did I get here?"

PROLOGUE

I have faced many difficulties as a mother from the moment my son was born. But I have to say that parenting a child with ADHD is the hardest yet most rewarding thing ever. I have learned a lot about my child and myself as a parent, but especially as a human. I documented my journey, including the good, the bad and the ugly, in the hopes that it would help other families to realise they are not alone in their struggles. I am excited to share the knowledge that empowered me, helped me find ways to love my child again, to know him, understand him and be more compassionate with him and myself.

Parenting isn't all hugs, kisses, and smiles. It can take a toll on us. The pressure of parenting, at times, can be so overwhelming that you may ask yourself, "Why is my child so difficult?" "Why can't he be like everyone else?" You may even find yourself wondering if a part of you hates your child. Societal norms do not typically approve of such feelings, so they are not openly acknowledged or discussed. Friends and family might judge us, and maybe even some of you, after reading my book, will judge me.

But I believe that such feelings are normal at times. It

doesn't mean that you no longer care about your child's well-being or you have given up on your commitment to protect them. Those moments don't make you a bad parent, they just prove you are human. What helped me was to acknowledge those feelings and not be ashamed of them. Change cannot happen until we are honest with ourselves. When I understood this, I realized that my child is not bad by default—something is causing him to behave this way. He must be going through something, and the only way to address it is to understand it.

PART 1

BECAUSE THE EASY WAY IS OVERRATED

Be Careful What You Wish For

When I was a child, dolls never quite captivated my interest like they did for my sisters and friends. Instead, I found solace and excitement in the world of books, where my imagination could take flight into fantastical realms. My dreams revolved around becoming an independent and successful woman—someone others would admire for all her achievements. Children and marriage were not part of my envisioned future.

That changed when I met Tom. From that moment, I couldn't imagine a single day without him by my side. My parents adored him, and he quickly became the son they never had—a breath of fresh air after raising three daughters!

Tom and I were visiting my parents one Christmas and it seemed like a usual seasonal gathering. To my surprise, Tom had chosen this special occasion to propose to me.

Afterwards, as we all sat around the table preparing to enjoy our Christmas dinner and celebrate our engagement, my dad suddenly stood up and asked for everyone's attention. He had a mischievous twinkle in his eye as he began his impromptu speech. Little did I know that what he was about to say would be engraved in our memories forever.

"I wish that next year there will be a small, tiny addition to the family sitting with us at this table," he announced with a grin. My heart skipped a beat as my dad's words sank in. For as long as I can remember, my life revolved around my career. From a young age, my dreams were filled with corner offices, high-powered meetings and accomplishments that echoed through the corporate world. I never envisioned myself settling down with a husband and starting a family. And here I was, sitting engaged to Tom, and my dad playfully proposing the idea of a baby. It was a moment of mixed emotions, where my past dreams intersected with the unexpected turns of the present, and my future was now uncharted territory. Even then, I still couldn't see children in my future.

Life has a way of introducing plot twists that we never see coming. One cold evening, with the wind and rain tapping against the window, I found myself gazing at a small plastic stick. Two pink lines stared back at me and my dreams shattered right in front of my eyes. I was pregnant.

My heart raced as I pondered the implications of this unexpected revelation. My mind, which was always an oasis of organised plans, strategies and visions, turned into a tornado of thoughts and emotions.

Now, with this life-altering news in my hands, I knew I had to share it with Tom, my soon-to-be husband. I was well aware that he shared my vision of a life filled with adventure, ambition and pursuit of professional success.

I finally mastered the courage to tell him.

"Tom, there is something I need to talk to you about."

"What's on your mind, love?"

I hesitated for a moment. "It is… it is big news. I don't even know how to say it."

"You are scaring me a little. What is going on?"

"I am pregnant."

"Are you sure?" he responded with his eyes wide open.

"Yes, I took a test and it is positive."

For a moment, the weight of the news hung in the air between us. Yet, as the minutes passed, a range of emotions flickered across his face—surprise, apprehension, and eventually, a glimmer of something else. Something that hinted at the possibility of embracing this new, uncharted chapter of our lives.

The next morning, I nervously picked up the phone to call my parents.

As I waited for the phone to connect, my mind raced through a tumultuous sea of thoughts. I questioned my ability to balance motherhood with my career. Would I have to re-evaluate my future plans?

Finally, the phone connected and my mom's voice filled the line. "Hello?"

"Hi, Mom," I replied nervously. "I have something to tell you and Dad."

"What is it?" she asked, sounding concerned.

'I... I am pregnant," I finally said.

"That's wonderful news! Anthony, come quick, your daughter is pregnant!"

Dad was as delighted as she was. "I didn't know that Christmas wishes could still come true," he said, laughing.

From the moment I took the pregnancy test and learned I was going to be a mom, my life took an unexpected turn. Suddenly, everything seemed uncertain. I felt like my entire world turned upside down and all my plans went out of the window in that moment.

But as the months passed and my belly grew, I began to embrace the idea of motherhood with joy and excitement.

At the same time, I refused to believe that becoming a mom meant giving up on my personal goals and ambitions. I wanted to have it all—a fulfilling career and a loving family. I was determined to prove it was possible to balance both worlds.

During my pregnancy, I remained dedicated to my career. I refused to let the impending arrival of my baby derail my aspirations. I vividly recall those moments in the office when I found myself racing up and down the stairs, striving to complete projects before my maternity leave began. The thought of stepping away from the office for an extended period weighed heavily on my mind, and I worried about missing out on significant opportunities.

The due date was approaching and I realized I didn't have any other choice but to step away from work. However, I was determined to return to work as soon as I could and resume my career. My female colleagues who were in similar positions used to tell me that I could not have it all and I would eventually have to choose between my career and motherhood. I was going to prove them wrong without a doubt. I could have it all. I could be a mother and have a successful career. There isn't a one-size-fits-all approach in this situation. Every woman is different when it comes to her career needs and her family. And that is fine. What was important to me was that there was no judgment or shame when it came to balancing motherhood with a career. I married a man who supports and encourages my career and personal choices. I was ready to accept that, some days, my balance would shift between the two.

Fairy Tale Turned Nightmare

Throughout my pregnancy, I watched movies and read books about delivery, immersing myself in the stories of other mothers welcoming their little ones into the world.

I could imagine the scene in the delivery room, the emotions filling the air as our baby made its grand entrance. The thought of holding our newborn, skin to skin, warmed by heart. I knew it would be an unforgettable moment that we would cherish forever.

Surprise! My delivery wasn't straightforward.

As I was in labour, my blood pressure went through the roof, so my doctor advised me to get an epidural as it would reduce my blood pressure. "Turn on your side and hold still. Do not move!" she said. Easier said than done when you are having contractions. I turned on my side and waited, gripping Tom's hand and bracing myself for the mother of all shots. I held my breath, closed my eyes and prayed that the next contraction wouldn't come until they finished. My friends warned me that the epidural hurts like hell. Some said that it was worse than childbirth. I felt a momentary burning sensation but very little pain. A few minutes after the epidural was administered, the heart rate monitor started beeping. "What is happening? Is it my blood pressure?" I asked. My blood pressure was dropping and my baby's heart rate was slowing down.

"I am sorry, but we cannot wait any longer. We have to perform an emergency C-section, the baby needs to come out!"

I saw Tom being pushed out of the room, the doctors and nurses running around, then I was being wheeled out of the room into an OR. Tears streamed down my cheeks. I was so scared, but I am not sure if I was scared for myself or my baby at that moment. Everything happened so fast. I felt panic. As I was being rolled over from my bed onto the operating table, I felt pain in my lower belly. "How is it possible? She just had an epidural... she shouldn't feel anything." My body wasn't fully numb. They had to put me under general anaesthesia to perform the C-section.

As I slowly awakened, I found myself in a small, unfamiliar room. The first thing my eyes fell upon was the comforting sight of my husband standing by my bedside, holding my hand. Confusion washed over me as I tried to piece together what had happened and if our baby was ok.

Then a nurse entered the room, carrying a tiny bundle wrapped in a blue and white-striped blanket with a little cotton beanie on his head. It was my baby boy. As I looked at his teeny red face, I searched for traces of myself and Tom in him. As I was holding him in my arms, I tried my best to feel the overwhelming love and connection that I anticipated. But at that moment, the feelings I had envisioned weren't there. I couldn't feel that immediate bond that I had heard other mothers talking about. It felt like someone went to a shop and got me a random baby. It didn't feel like mine. That afternoon, a few of my closest friends arrived. Their presence was comforting, especially since my family wasn't there yet. Together, we gazed at the tiny human being before us, cherishing the bonds of friendships that made this day even more special. Towards the end of visiting hours, I started feeling increasingly unwell. My temperature spiked, I had horrible chest pains and difficulty breathing. The doctors came to check on me. Their initial suspicion was that I had developed a urinary tract infection, bladder infection or even a kidney infection.

As the days went by, the doctors and nurses continued their efforts to diagnose and treat my condition. They took my blood multiple times, hoping to find what was making me so unwell. However, my veins were barely visible, making it difficult for them to draw blood.

Each attempt felt like a game of chance, with more misses than hits.

The doctor would insert the needle and sit there, looking for my veins, tapping his fingers on the inside of my elbow. No blood. "I am sorry, I have to try this again." And off he went again, trying to insert the needle into something that he believed to be a vein. The needle was in my arm, and he kept looking for the vein. I could feel the uncomfortable pinching and turning of the needle in my arm and then... nothing. Finally, he asked a nurse to come in to assist. She had better luck than him.

The next day, I saw the doctor coming again with a small tray containing some vials and syringes. "Please, not again!" But they had to. My condition wasn't improving and they needed to keep testing my blood. After a few days, they made the decision to insert a cannula into my arm, which was supposed to make the process easier. And it did... for a couple of days. Then the cannula kept falling out and we were back where we started. My condition was deteriorating and we still had no clue what was causing my fever. As taking blood was difficult for them, they had to draw blood from the top of my hands, my wrists and between my toes. When that wasn't enough, the doctor suggested taking blood from my groin. My eyes almost popped out of my head when I heard that, but I was too weak to protest. There were nurses around me, holding my arms and my legs to make sure I didn't move. Then I felt the needle being inserted into my groin. I felt shooting pain and couldn't bear it. I screamed out loud, "Stop! Stop!" It felt like I was being tortured. I looked and felt like a pin cushion.

Every day, I was getting weaker and weaker and I wasn't capable of taking care of my child. I had dark circles beneath my eyes, no appetite, and I felt detached as if I was watching myself. Everything that I was going through didn't seem real. It felt like a long and horrifying nightmare and I was hoping that any minute I would wake up from it and all would be ok again.

The nurses came every day with my son, Jack, for me to breastfeed him. But I couldn't. They kept reminding me of how important breastfeeding was for the baby. "Try again," the nurse said for the tenth time. "Try to relax!" I was barely holding on to my life and they were asking me to relax? I hated those moments. I was desperate. I had to feed my son, but I couldn't. I have never been so sick. All I wanted was some rest and to get better. The child felt like a burden to me—another thing that I needed to take care of when I wasn't able to take care of myself. It was distracting me from getting better!

Since I was pumped full of antibiotics and had no milk, they finally decided to use formula to feed Jack.

A moment of relief. The child's care was finally not my responsibility and I could rest. The nurses and my husband were feeding him, changing him and taking care of him. Tom went to work every morning, and then from work, straight to the hospital to take care of Jack and to spend time with me. Tom is naturally tall and has a very slim build. But the man who visited me daily was disappearing in front of my eyes. Drawn face, sunken features and very noticeable dark circles under his eyes. He looked worried and exhausted. But he always had a smile for me.

One evening, while I was lying in bed, I overheard a conversation between the nurses in the hallway that scared me, "I hope she won't die on us here. This is the maternity ward, babies are born here, people don't die here." Was there a chance I could actually die? During that time, I didn't even think of the baby, I just thought about myself. What do I need to do to get better and back on my feet? I am not a person who just gives up… what do I need to do to fight?" If they just sent me home, my mom would make me her chicken soup and everything would get better like it always did when I was a child. But nobody was letting me go home. And I doubted that chicken soup was the magic cure I was hoping for. I felt helpless and lonely. A time that was supposed to be one of the happiest moments in my life had turned into a complete nightmare.

My parents came to help Tom and a decision was

made to send Jack home with them as he was healthy and didn't need to be in the hospital. Then, finally, a diagnosis arrived. "You have pneumonia." They prescribed another set of antibiotics, but these didn't work either. A new doctor was called in—some kind of specialist. He determined it could be pulmonary edema. "You have too much fluid in your lungs. We have to drain the fluid as soon as possible, otherwise, you could drown." A couple of hours later, I was scheduled for a procedure.

"Sit up, place your hands on your thighs and keep looking straight ahead," the doctor said. I made a mistake and turned around. There, I saw a doctor with the biggest needle I have ever seen. "Is he planning to treat a horse with this?" I thought to myself. But to be honest, I didn't care anymore, I just wanted to get it over with, feel better and go home. He administered a local anaesthetic somewhere around my ribs.

"Don't worry, you won't feel any pain." Oh, boy, was he wrong! As soon as he inserted the needle, I felt incredible pain and pressure as he slowly withdrew the fluid. I screamed so loud and for so long that I am sure people on the streets could hear me. It felt like years passed before it was finally over. I was sent to bed to rest. Over the next few days, I started feeling better and more like myself again. Finally, a month after my son was born, I was allowed to go home.

Lost in Mom Translation

Sitting in the car as Tom drove me home, all I wanted was to see and hold my child. When the moment finally arrived, I looked into his eyes and wondered what I was feeling. I had this idea that the minute I locked eyes with my baby, I would fall in love and feel that love more strongly than ever before. That is what I had seen in the movies... what I had read about in the books and magazines. Where is that moment? Why is it not happening for me? I carried this child for nine months, so there should be some connection, some bond, even the tiniest spark of love and excitement. I felt so many emotions, but none of them really resembled love. I felt cheated.

What had I done?! My old life had literally vanished in an instant. My identity, dreams, hopes, future... my entire life all irrevocably changed. I knew somewhere deep down that it was all for the better, but in that moment, all I could feel was loss, fear, and honestly, even a little bit of resentment. Because of this tiny human being, I had suffered for over a month in a hospital—almost died. And here I am now and he is expecting me to love him and take care of him?

At that moment, I came to a terrible realisation. I was a bad mom... I should never have become a mother.

Every new mother I spoke to would go on and on about how much they loved their child and how easy and natural it felt to them. I was officially a horrible person and the worst mom on Earth.

The first time Jack smiled at me definitely started to help me like him more. But, then again, he smiled at any person who came to visit us and made funny faces or noises at him. And let's not forget every time he farted put a smile on his face too. Each day felt the same. My son was becoming cuter and cuter, but I still didn't feel that connection I kept hoping for. I worked hard to take care of him and yet there was no sign of affection or love. I felt so ashamed of it and never shared these feelings with anyone. I spent weeks thinking that there was something wrong with me.

Then it happened! When Jack was about five months old, he was sitting in my mother's arms as I walked into the room. When he saw me, he gave me such a big smile and leaned towards me. My mom said, "Oh, look, he knows his mommy is here," and that simple sentence was what I had been waiting for. From there on out, bonding with him and loving him became second nature. I felt like loving Jack wasn't something that came naturally to me, but I learned to love him.

Every month of his life became more fun and I thought that the hard part was over and I would never doubt my love for him ever again. When Jack was six months old, my mom went home. Oh, I should have mentioned... my parents live in a different country and she was here only to help us out while I was recovering and to ensure that I had the support I needed during the first months of being a new mom.

Despite my feelings—or the lack thereof—at the beginning, Jack was an amazing baby. He slept through the night, ate and slept again. I was slowly but surely getting bored at home and I couldn't wait to go back to work and resume my career. I was restless, and every day felt the same. I longed to be challenged, have opportunities to learn new things, interact with people and feel a sense of purpose again. When Jack was about seven months old, I decided to return to work. On his first day going to kindergarten, I was worried about how he would react. But it turned out the transition was much harder for me!

We handed him over to the teachers. "Say bye to Mommy," the teacher said and waved at me with Jack's hand and closed the door behind them. I stood there at the door waiting to see if he would start crying. And part of me was hoping he would, that he would miss me and would need me. But he didn't.

I remember the jittery excitement, the butterflies in my stomach the night before the first day back at school when I was a child. Going back to work provoked similar emotions with so many things to look forward to. I couldn't wait to get my career back on track, find my old self again, face new challenges, solve issues and have adult conversations. I couldn't wait to be 'me' again!

I returned to work and Jack spent time playing with kids his age and he enjoyed every moment of it. Every day I got a report from kindergarten about what he did, ate, and how many times he pooped. Yes, it was that detailed. They played a lot of games with him, which supported his development. He arrived home with pictures he had painted as well as his foot and finger prints. I was sure I had made the right decision to send him to kindergarten at such an early age as I wouldn't have ever done those things at home with him. Every day, both of us returned home with big smiles on our faces. And I felt like myself again!

PART 2

NAVIGATING THE WILD TERRAIN AND THE BATTLE OF WILLS

He Will Grow Out Of It

We all really enjoyed the next few years, watching Jack take his first steps, learning to ride his first bike, expressing his wants and needs and starting to form his individual personality. From the time he could walk, he was always on the move. Even sitting at the dinner table was hard for him and he always needed to move or fidget. Tom used to say to me, "That's because you couldn't sit still when you were pregnant with him."

Jack was active, curious, bright and energetic. He always had a way of putting a smile on our faces. We had so many laughs together because of his mischievous personality.

Everyone would describe Jack as very kind. He always wanted to help his friends and teachers and he didn't like sitting quietly and being bored. I never considered that there could be something different about him. We were a happy family... for the time being. When he was around three years old, my parents visited us again and we went out for dinner.

We sat down at the table, and within a few minutes, Jack was fidgeting in his seat. He grabbed the salt and pepper shakers and started playing with them and pretending they were race cars. I kept taking them away from him. "These are not toys, please leave them alone." I turned away for just a second when I heard someone next to us scolding Jack for pulling things from their table. I instantly felt ashamed. I looked at him, and with a firm voice, asked, "What are you doing? I told you to stop and sit quietly." Suddenly, it felt like everyone in the restaurant was looking at us. The feeling of shame was joined by guilt and fear—feelings I was very familiar with. I had experienced them before, especially after Jack was born when I struggled to bond with him in the way I thought I should. Those emotions had taken hold of me then, just as they did now. It got to the point where I was too embarrassed to finish our dinner and decided to leave the restaurant. I couldn't understand why Jack behaved the way he did. I thought he was just a boy who always needed to move and play with something and that, one day, he would grow out of it.

Boredom Meets Education

Big and new steps in children's lives create big and new feelings, and not just for children, but for parents as well. His first school day came faster than we thought possible. The mix of pride and nostalgia swelled within me as he stood there in his school uniform. The school bag on his back seemed as if it could have carried him. It was a poignant moment, a visual reminder of how quickly he was growing up, and it tugged at my heartstrings in a way only a parent could understand. Jack was always very independent, and his first day of school was no different. We walked him into his class and spent a few minutes with him. He suddenly waved us goodbye, a smile lighting up his face, and then he didn't look back. His first school day was a success. He came home smiling, recounting the adventures of his day. It was evident that he had embraced this new chapter with a sense of wonder and curiosity. His eyes sparkled with enthusiasm as he shared stories of making new friends, exploring the classroom, and even proudly mentioned that he had managed to tie his shoelaces all by himself. His enthusiasm was infectious, filling the house with an air of excitement and anticipation for the next day's adventures.

* * *

The next few years in primary school went really well.

The learning environment was very playful—they were moving a lot and he really enjoyed it.

However, when Jack moved into the older classes, the school's expectations changed and the rules became stricter. Children were expected to sit still, pay attention in class, do their school work quietly and play nicely with their friends at recess. For the first time, we received a request to visit the school. When I walked into the classroom, Jack's teacher, Ms Murphy, smiled at me. But it didn't seem to me like a genuine smile. She sat at a table and offered us a small wooden chair. I felt like an oversized child in that tiny chair, hoping I would be able to get back out of it! It was normal for teachers to meet with parents, but this time, it felt different. She pulled out some papers with notes and smiled. "Right, thank you very much for coming today," she said. "Before we get started, do you have any questions for me about Jack?" I was sure I had questions, but at that moment, I couldn't remember them. I just kept wondering why she was being so serious. She hadn't even asked us how we were doing.

"I don't really have any questions; I am just wondering if everything is ok?" I said.

"We have some concerns about your son's academic performance and behaviour," she answered while shifting between her papers.

"Ok..." I responded hesitantly, not knowing what would come next.

"He is a very bright and kind child, full of energy, but his behaviour is becoming a concern for us." She shifted in her seat again like she was uncomfortable with the message she was delivering. "He is disruptive in class, he keeps moving around without permission and now he is even involving other students. When we call him out, he just makes an inappropriate joke about it." I kept staring at her with a very serious face. "Maybe this is something that you need to discuss with him at home as it is becoming more frequent. He has such huge potential, but he keeps rushing his school work and not checking for mistakes. It seems like he doesn't care, he is disorganized, always forgetting something and very easily distracted. He acts in a childish and immature way. Myself and other teachers believe that this is something that needs to be addressed at the earliest."

I paused for a second, thinking about what to say. "Thank you for your feedback, we will discuss this at home with Jack." I gathered my purse and coat that was hanging at the back of my tiny chair and left the school a bit shocked. My son acts in a childish way? He is a 10-year-old child, how else is he supposed to act? I was confused, but also disappointed. As I walked home, I thought about what to say to Jack. When I opened the door, Jack came running towards me.

"Hi, Mom, what did the teacher say?" He knew about the meeting and was curious to find out what had been discussed.

"Maybe we should have dinner first and then we can sit down and talk about it."

Jack sighed and agreed.

"Come, sit next to me," I said to him as I settled into the sofa in the living room.

"How was school today?" I asked.

"Boring," he replied.

"What did you do today?"

"Nothing."

"You must have done something; you were there for six hours."

Jack just looked at me like I had two heads. "Nothing, Mom, school is soooo boring."

"As you know, I met with Ms Murphy today. She said that you are very kind and energetic. And that sometimes because of all that energy, you cannot sit still."

"Yeah, because there is nothing to do and I am bored."

"But you do have things to do during class, don't you? What are the other children doing?"

"But I always finish first and then I have nothing to do."

"Could you maybe ask Ms Murphy to give you some extra work?"

"She did, but I don't want to."

"So, what do you do when you are done with your work?"

"I talk to my friends."

"But you understand that they might be still focusing on getting their work done. And that could be disturbing them and others in the class."

"Yeah, but school is so booooring, Mom."

I assumed that what the teacher highlighted was due to boredom and Jack not being challenged enough. The next day, Ms Murphy and I agreed that Jack would be given some extra activities to challenge him a bit more.

However, his behaviour continued to cause problems. We were receiving regular phone calls from school and noticed a shift in his behaviour at home. He was becoming more argumentative and becoming frustrated and angry very easily when things didn't go his way. We tried punishments for poor behaviour and rewards for good behaviour.

We tried to explain how his actions impacted others and we hoped he would learn from his mistakes. But that wasn't the case. We loved our child and wanted to help him, but in those moments, we felt ashamed of him.

Fleeting Victories

The more we tried to help him, the more frustrated he became.

The happy child was turning into an angry child in front of our eyes. We decided to seek professional help. A friend of ours recommended a play therapist, Laurie.

Laurie was in her late 20s and had a kind but still very childlike way about her. The initial consultation took place in Laurie's office. As soon as we arrived, she opened the door and welcomed us. "Hi, you must be Jack's parents. I am Laurie, so lovely to meet you."

Her office was small, with beige walls and a big window at the back. Underneath the window was a sandbox with different toys. The walls were lined with shelves. On each shelf were different toys, therapy putties… things needed to make slime and who knows what else. On one side of the room, I noticed a play kitchen with a tiny tea set. Laurie's wooden desk was in the corner. "Please sit," she said. "First, I would like to get to know more about Jack if that is ok with you. Please tell me about him." It was an opportunity for us to finally vent. We started describing the challenges we had been facing and how Jack's behaviour impacted his academic performance. As we moved on to discuss the feedback we received from his teachers, she interrupted us. "I understand that this must be very hard for you and Jack. What would you say if we just put those things on hold for a moment and maybe start with Jack's strengths? What would you consider to be his strengths?" That question surprised us. We paused for a second and I sighed. Why can't I think of any strengths? I am sure he has some, so why am I not able to think of any? After a second or two, I blurted out, "Kindness! Jack is very kind."

Tom added, "Also very playful and energetic." She smiled as we started to list out his strengths. Somehow, it all became so much easier once we started. She took down his developmental history and explained how the play therapy worked.

"I will start the first session with a short and lovely story. This story will include Jack and the reasons why he is coming to see me. We will meet weekly for the next six weeks, followed by a review session with you. As we play together, we will identify and work through some emotional conflicts that might be hard for him to express verbally. By playing and using pretend scenarios, children tend to be more comfortable talking about their difficulties." Everything she said made sense to me, so I couldn't have been happier with our decision to approach her.

"Do you have any questions for me?" she asked.

"Jack is 10, do you think that the toys and games you have here will be suitable for him?"

She smiled as she responded. "I work with children up to 14 years old. And so far, each one of them has found something of interest here. But if he would like to bring some things from home to play with instead, he can do that too." We really liked her. She was very kind, understanding, and had such a warmth to her. Sometimes you meet a person and they have such a positive and calming presence. You feel safe, understood and cared for when you're with them. You know what I mean.

* * *

Jack spent almost two months in play therapy. He developed a great relationship with Laurie and really liked seeing her. The session to review Jack's progress was approaching. I was so nervous going into that meeting. While we were waiting outside her office, my husband sat on a chair and I kept pacing up and down the corridor. Then the door opened. "Hello, how are you doing?" she said with a huge smile on her face and welcomed us into her office. As we sat down, she looked at me and said, "You look very nervous, there is no need to be," she reassured me. "Jack is an amazing child, very bright and so smart. You were worried about him not being able to enjoy the toys and games available here," she said. I smiled as she continued talking. "We spent the majority of the time playing together in the sandbox and making tea in the play kitchen." My face must have said it all because then she added, "Don't be so surprised... when children feel safe, they can do what they need, not what we expect of them." I took a deep breath. "I have been observing him for the past few weeks while we were playing, but also having conversations with him. I have noticed that he has developmental delay, specifically around his emotional maturity. He is 10, but when he feels safe, he acts and behaves like a four or five-year-old. We had opportunities to talk about progress he made so far and acknowledge that even if it sometimes seemed that we were just playing, we were actually doing some hard work and Jack should be very proud of himself." Laurie recommended that we continue to observe him at home and continue to be more playful with him. She said we should consider how we would play, talk and interact with a five-year-old. To meet his emotional needs, it would be very important to continue this practice at home as well. We agreed that we would pause these sessions for now and see how we got along at home. Laurie reassured us that she would always be available to help and support us. When we left, I couldn't help but feel responsible and guilty for the emotional delay in Jack's development. I had completely failed my son and I was the one who had done this to him. I was a bad mother and I had no clue what I was doing. Did it matter that everything I did was done with the best intentions and out of love? It didn't change the fact that we were in this situation and our son was facing all these challenges. Maybe I could have done something to prevent this.

For the next couple of weeks, we did exactly as Laurie suggested and saw some improvements in his behaviour. But the progress did not last for long.

The Principal's Frequent Flyer Program

The end of August brought that dreaded 'back to school' feeling. While this can be an exciting time for many, for some, it can be very stressful. We were relieved that school was starting again as we didn't have to entertain Jack and deal with his daily outbursts. We hoped we could split the load with his teachers, but moving from primary school to a secondary school is a big step. Children are no longer the 'big fish' in primary school. Instead, they are the 'little' first-year students again. This can bring a sense of uncertainty—new school, new faces, new subjects, different rules (often very strict rules), peer pressure and the children have no choice but to adapt. That meant Jack needed to make new friends. And the best way to make a name for himself in class as well as in school was to cause trouble. Not even a week had passed before the school principal requested to meet with us.

The meeting was scheduled for 9.45 am. The entire morning, I had butterflies in my stomach. I couldn't stop pacing around the house. School had just started and we were heading for the principal's office already. I walked to school on my own as Tom needed to work. He wished me good luck as he was leaving and asked me to call him as soon as the meeting was over.

As I stepped into the school, the vastness of the halls immediately caught my attention. The space seemed much more expansive than Jack's primary school. After I announced myself at the reception, I patiently waited for the principal. "Good morning, my name is Mr McCarthy," he introduced himself as he shook my hand. In his 50s, he exuded a sense of professionalism and poise. With an average height and build, he projected an air of authority and approachability at the same time.

"Please come with me," Mr McCarthy said, gesturing for me to follow him. As we walked through the big and elongated hallways, I couldn't help but notice the walls decorated with numerous pictures showcasing the students' impressive work. It was evident that the school took great pride in fostering creativity and academic excellence.

As Mr McCarthy opened the door to his office, I noticed

a woman sitting at a small round table with four chairs. She had short brown hair and a warm smile on her face. Mr McCarthy introduced us, "This is Ms Walsh. Jack's Year Head. Please sit," he said, pulling up a chair for me.

"Thank you very much for coming. We asked you here today to talk about Jack. We know that, for some students, the transition between primary and secondary school can be hard, so we thought it would be best if we got together to discuss how we can help him," Ms Walsh said in a warm and understanding tone.

Mr McCarthy chimed in, "Starting a new school can be overwhelming and we want to ensure that Jack feels comfortable and supported in every way possible."

"What do you mean by difficult transitions, did something happen?" I asked.

"Jack has been distracting other students. He wants to be the centre of attention and not in a good way. He cracks jokes, doesn't listen and talks back at his teachers." I listened attentively as they laid out their concerns about Jack's behaviour. My face flushed with a combination of embarrassment and worry. It wasn't easy to hear that my son was being disruptive and not making a positive impression at his new school.

"I... I had no idea that Jack was behaving this way," I admitted, trying to compose myself. "But I appreciate you bringing this to my attention," I continued with a mix of concern and determination. "I have noticed some changes in Jack's behaviour at home, but I didn't realize it was affecting his school life to his extent."

Ms Walsh nodded empathetically, "Transitions can be challenging, and it is not uncommon for students to act out in response to new environments."

"I agree," Mr McCarthy added. "Our focus here is to support Jack and provide him with the tools to navigate through this adjustment period successfully."

Feeling a sense of responsibility, I asked, "What can we do to help him overcome these challenges? I want him to thrive and make positive connections with his peers as well as his teachers."

"We believe open communication is key," Ms Walsh replied. "Let's work together to establish clear expectations for Jack's behaviour."

Mr McCarthy added, "Additionally, we can collaborate with his teachers to create a positive reinforcement system, acknowledging his efforts when he displays good behaviour and redirecting him when necessary."

Feeling reassured by their support, I left the meeting with a renewed sense of hope. I was determined to help Jack navigate through this challenging phase.

As I left the meeting, I couldn't shake the feeling of unease. I had hoped for a more positive start to Jack's secondary school journey.

I knew it was essential to have an open and honest conversation with him, creating a safe space for him to share his feelings and experiences.

Walking back home, my mind raced with thoughts of how best to approach the conversation. I wanted him to know that I cared deeply for him, but also that there were certain rules and expectations that needed to be followed.

Once Jack got home from school, I looked for the right moment to sit down with him. "Hey," I began gently. "I had a meeting with your principal and Year Head today. They mentioned that there were some issues at school."

Jack looked at me with a mixture of surprise and uncertainty on his face.

I began by emphasizing the importance of listening in class. "When our teacher talks, it's essential to listen," I said. "If they ask you a question, answer, give them your full attention and respond respectfully."

Jack nodded. "I know sometimes it is hard to focus, especially with so much going on around you. But can you try?" I asked.

"I will try, Mom."

A week later, my phone rang. I saw the school number popping up on my screen. For a second, I hesitated to pick up. "What now?" I thought to myself.

"Hello, how are you?" Ms Walsh announced herself. This time, she had no concerns to report, but she had a question about Jack's well-being. "Why? Is he ok?" I was surprised by her inquiry.

Ms Walsh explained, "The teachers have noticed that he is taking multiple bathroom breaks during class. We wanted to make sure he is feeling well and there is nothing affecting his comfort and concentration."

I hadn't been aware of this but I assured her, "I will definitely check with him as soon as he gets home. Thank you for bringing this to my attention."

When Jack got home from school, I sat down with him and asked about the frequent bathroom breaks. Jack hesitated for a moment before replying. "I don't need to pee, Mom. But school is just so boring, I go to the bathroom so I don't have to sit in the class."

How can he be bored? New school, new subjects, new teachers... he even has different teachers for each class. How can that be boring?

We agreed that he would try his best to stay in class and take his bathroom breaks during break times.

We managed to make it through a couple of weeks without any phone calls from the school, then Ms Walsh called again. I braced myself for the conversation ahead.

"Hi, this is Ms Walsh, do you have a minute?" she inquired.

"Of course," I replied, trying to stay calm despite my apprehension.

"Jack pushed another student during recess."

"I am sorry to hear that, I will discuss this with him," I replied, trying to remain composed.

Ms Walsh continued, "We take the safety and well-being of all of our students very seriously, and pushing others can lead to accidents."

"I completely understand," I said with remorse and a sense of responsibility to address this at the earliest.

Over dinner that evening, I approached this topic with Jack gently. "How was school today? Did anything interesting happen?" I asked.

"Nothing, Mom," he responded.

"Ms Walsh called… is there something you want to share? I really would like to hear your side of the story."

He looked at me, surprised that I knew about it, and started to justify his actions. "We were waiting in front of the classroom for like forever. It was so boring. And my friend and I were joking, he was messing up my hair and I was messing up his and then we pushed each other. Not a big deal, Mom, it was just for fun."

I listened and tried to understand his perspective.

"I see," I replied. "I can see how waiting in front of the classroom can be boring. And I understand that you just wanted to have fun with your friend, but we need to remember that even when we are joking around, we shouldn't do anything that may accidentally hurt someone, like pushing someone."

"Ok, Mom," Jack responded as he got up from the table and headed to his room.

One morning, I decided to sleep in as I hadn't slept well the night before. I woke up to a missed phone call and a voicemail. Ms Walsh was requesting a meeting with me and the principal. My heart skipped a beat as I wondered what could have prompted a meeting with the principal.

The next morning, I marched into the school and found myself sitting in the principal's office once again.

"Jack has been forgetting his homework, his school books are damaged and they need to be paid for. He continues to disturb the class. He is becoming very rude and disrespectful towards his teachers, and that is something we cannot accept."

Here we go again... I could only apologise and assure them that I would talk to Jack and do my best to address it.

This time, I wasn't as understanding as before. I felt quite upset that I had to apologize for him once again.

When I told Jack that I was at the school and explained the feedback I received, his only response was, "I don't care!"

Not what I expected and I felt feelings of frustration taking over me. "Maybe if you cared a bit more, you wouldn't forget your homework, and your books would be still intact," I responded with a raised voice.

"I don't care, Mom!" he yelled back at me and left.

A Mom's Serenade

When I was going to school, my parents always told me, "Start the school year the way you want to continue." And boy, did Jack live by that mantra! The way he started the school year was the way he continued it. Regular phone calls, regular meetings with the principal, listening to the same stories, and at home having the same conversations over and over again. According to Jack, nothing was his fault—there was always someone else to blame. His academic performance kept declining. Teachers could see his potential, but he wasn't living up to it. There were some subjects that he enjoyed and did well in, and teachers kept questioning why he did so well in that topic but not in another one.

When I explored it with Jack, he provided a surprisingly reasonable answer, "I can concentrate well if what they are talking about is interesting. But if I find it boring, I can't."

We all know that school often entails learning about topics that may not be of interest to us, but we still had to learn about them. Hence, we wondered why Jack couldn't grasp this concept, especially considering his obvious potential.

I was also aware of the fact that once you get labelled as the 'problem child' at school, regardless of the situation, you often become the primary focus of attention.

Even though I was hurting inside and feeling embarrassed, I wanted to be on Jack's side. My goal was to offer him support. If he didn't feel supported at school or by his friends, I wanted him to know that he could always count on his parents. And I was able to maintain this approach for a while, but his behaviour started to escalate and the problems got bigger and bigger until I could no longer let things continue without trying something—anything—to fix it.

* * *

At home, he started having emotional tantrums. I was convinced that, at school, in front of his friends, he was trying to keep his emotions under control and keep his 'cool', and this was the reason behind his emotional outbursts when he got home.

Every time he didn't get what he wanted or things were not going his way, he threw a tantrum. These tantrums became more and more frequent and intense. They started to dominate our lives. He wasn't just yelling and screaming. When he wanted something, he would beg and beg. "Mom, please. Mom, I beg you. Mom, please," and that would go on for hours. We had been told by the therapist that we should ignore it. That if he saw it wasn't working, he would stop. He didn't.

One evening while sitting in front of the TV, he asked if he could go on his computer. He asked nicely, and I responded, "It is too late, honey, it is almost your bedtime, so you should get ready for bed."

Unhappy with my response, Jack persisted, asking repeatedly to go on his computer. And as I wasn't budging, he started to get more and more emotional. I tried to tell him that I love him and hold him, but in this emotional state, he wasn't listening to anything I said. As his frustration grew, he resorted to crying and repeating his request on a never-ending loop. "Mom, please! Mom, I beg you! Mom, please! Mom, I beg you! Mom, please! Mom, please! Mom, I beg you! Mom, please!" When he realized his pleas weren't having the desired effect, he resorted to poking me with his little finger. These tiny jabs felt like needles hitting my arm at a very fast speed. Still, I attempted to remain calm and stand my ground, not giving in to his demands.

However, after enduring three hours of the continuous cycle of hearing "Mom, please! Mom, I beg you! Mom, please!" my patience reached its limits and I started yelling at him. My response only seemed to reinforce his behaviour as it showed that what he was doing was provoking a reaction. So, he kept going with the poking and repeating, "Mom, please! Mom, I beg you! Mom, please!"

As it was already past midnight, I decided to go to bed with the hope that Jack would do the same. However, he followed me into the bedroom and continued his persistent behaviour of poking and begging. Around 3 am, both of us were exhausted and Jack finally drifted off to sleep next to me. As I closed my eyes, I held onto the hope that the next morning would bring a fresh start. That hope was interrupted as I woke up to the sharp sensation of poking. Opening my eyes, I found Jack sitting next to me, repeating his pleas.

As it was a school day, I told him that he would get his computer time after school, just to get him to go.

As soon as Jack left the house, my mind couldn't help but replay the exhausting scenario from the previous night. I found myself analysing how I could have handled it differently. I felt mixed emotions. I was angry at him for his persistence and upset with myself for eventually giving in.

The few hours of peace and quiet while he was at school were a relief, but they also filled me with anxiety and fear as the school day approached its end.

The moment Jack came home, he wanted to go and play computer games with his friend. My attempt to explain the importance of doing his homework first seemed futile. As soon as he sensed my efforts to convince him otherwise, the tantrums would start and I found myself giving in to his demands.

"Go on your PC and we will do the homework after," I said, feeling a sense of defeat. Deep down, I knew that by backing down, I had undermined my own authority as a parent. But at that moment, I couldn't handle another tantrum.

I never thought that the word 'Mom' could become an intense emotional trigger for me. Regardless of Jack's mood when he said it, the word seemed to carry all the weight of past struggles, the distress and frustration. Whenever I heard it, my heart would race and my body would react as if I was in danger. It felt as though my fists were clenching instinctively—a physical response to the emotional turmoil the word 'Mom' brought up.

Whenever Jack asked for something and I knew that my answer would be a 'no', my body would tremble and fear would consume me, dreading the prospect of another tantrum. My life felt like I was constantly tiptoeing around a potential outburst, walking on eggshells.

Not only was I afraid of the potential tantrums, but I also feared my own reactions. In those moments, I didn't recognize myself, how I was feeling or what I was thinking. In those challenging times, I felt desperate for it all to stop. Feelings of despair mixed with feelings of anger. There were fleeting instances when I was worried that I would do something drastic just to bring a momentary pause to the chaos. Under normal circumstances, the idea of raising a hand to my child would be unthinkable, but the intensity of my emotions and the fear of what I could be capable of was very unsettling. I knew that submitting to such impulses would lead to remorse and I wouldn't be able to forgive myself. It required every ounce of strength and determination to keep my emotions under control.

* * *

I just wanted my 12-year-old to work with me. I didn't expect him to blindly do exactly what I asked, I just didn't want him to work against me. But everything became a fight. He fought me every step of the way, from getting out of bed in the morning to getting dressed, brushing his teeth, doing his homework or eating dinner in the evening. He needed constant reminders of what needed to happen, and even with those reminders, he didn't do half of the things or lied about doing them.

Whether in the morning or evening, when we asked him if he had brushed his teeth or taken a shower, his response was always, "Yes."

But we didn't hear the shower running, and when we checked, the shower was completely dry—not a single drop of water to be found. His toothbrush showed no signs of use either. His go-to excuse was always, "I forgot."

His room was messy and disorganised. Despite our efforts to wash and iron his clothes, they never seemed to make it past the first step leading up to his room. They would pile up there, mixing with the dirty laundry.

Whenever we asked him to bring down his dirty laundry for washing, he would simply grab the entire stack, including freshly folded clothes from the previous week.

The pattern of forgetfulness and dishonesty became a recurring challenge, leaving us frustrated and concerned about his inability to take responsibility for his daily routines, in addition to the challenges we were already facing.

When I asked him to do something and pushed him

too hard, he would respond with an aggressive attitude and get really angry. "I am not doing it! I don't care!"

Despite our efforts to set rules, it seemed like they were only there for Jack to break. We engaged in numerous conversations with him, attempting to involve him in the rulemaking process so he would understand the reasoning behind them.

We all gathered at the table, aiming to have a productive conversation, but I found it very challenging to concentrate on what I was saying. My attention kept shifting to Jack, who was hanging from the chair, upside down. "Please sit up and pay attention to what we are saying," I would say, but that often resulted in him becoming annoyed or dismissive.

We tried to do it in the living room, in a more relaxed environment, but he would hang upside down from the sofa or constantly move, hiding under a blanket. It seemed that he wasn't interested in listening to us at all. Me repeating, "Please sit up! Please look at me when I am talking to you!" got us nowhere. We seemed to have hit a wall.

And whatever we managed to agree on, Jack would often deny or manipulate. His ability to twist things to suit his needs or conveniently forget prior agreements became a recurring pattern. To avoid misunderstandings and disagreements, we began writing down the outcomes of our conversations, hoping that having a clear record would help. However, even with written agreements, he managed to find loopholes and creative ways to disregard them.

His skill at finding solutions and reading between the lines, while impressive, presented us with many challenges. It sometimes felt as though he could be a lawyer, with his quick thinking and ability to navigate around the rules and expectations we had set.

* * *

My days were filled with constant reminders for seemingly mundane tasks and a constant fear of inadvertently saying something wrong.

Determined to find a solution, I delved into online research, reading numerous books on dealing with difficult and defiant children. I experimented with different communication techniques, hoping to find a better way to get through to Jack.

Traditional parenting strategies, which often worked with other children, fell short with Jack. Consistency and discipline didn't yield the desired results. Rewards and punishments failed to motivate him to improve his behaviour. In fact, he seemed to view punishment as a challenge to overcome rather than a reason to change. We were constantly in the process of trial and error. Failed attempts at discipline were the norm. Defeat was my reality.

Whatever we tried, it worked only for about a week or two before he cleverly manipulated the rules. The constant cycle of laying down rules, trying to empathize with his point of view and exhausting every strategy I learned left me feeling drained and frustrated.

I often found myself wondering why I wasn't one of those lucky parents with an easy and well-behaved child.

Listening to my friends share stories of their children's accomplishments and pride in them, I realized how envious I was. I tried to shift my focus to the positives, seeking reasons to be grateful for my child. There were moments when I couldn't find anything nice to say about him, and the feeling of pride had become a distant memory.

PART 3
ORDINARY IS OVERRATED

In Pursuit of Answers

As we reached our breaking point, the desperation to find a solution was overshadowed by a sense of shame and inadequacy. I was so reluctant to expose (what I saw as) our inability to raise our child properly. However, in our pursuit of answers, I stumbled across an article describing the challenges faced by parents of children with ADHD. The similarities to Jack's behaviour were uncanny and a glimmer of hope emerged. Could he possibly have ADHD?

Deep down, I knew that it was time to confront the issue and get him evaluated.

I was worried about what a diagnosis would mean. I didn't want my child to be labelled, but I knew that we needed help. "I don't see how it can hurt to have him tested," I said to Tom. "The assessment could provide an explanation for us and strategies to support him."

The appointment with the psychologist, Dr Dylan,

was a pivotal moment for us. The first thing he asked us to do was fill out an assessment together with Jack. As we were filling it out, all of the questions brought back memories of him not being able to sit still, sustain focus for extended periods of time, and the constant fidgeting and impulsivity.

Dr Dylan's small office was in a very big building. As I walked through the corridor, I caught glimpses of people sitting at their desks with headphones on through big glass windows. Dr Dylan introduced himself and asked, "Is there something specific you are concerned about?" "ADHD," I said, rubbing my sweaty hands.

"Ok, how long have you been concerned?" he asked, looking at the completed assessment we brought him.

"I would say we had general concerns about him since primary school, but just recently, we thought that it could be ADHD."

Dr Dylan attentively listened as we shared challenges we had been experiencing with Jack. He was interested to know if Jack was getting easily frustrated, irritated or even quick to rage. "Yes, we have seen some signs recently."

The doctor noted down something on his papers. "Anything else you want me to look at?" he asked.

"His academic performance has been sliding," I

replied. "His handwriting is not great and his verbal comprehension is also pretty weak." He then asked about family history and explained the testing process to us. He needed information from Jack's teachers and also requested to meet with Jack for an hour to run through some tests.

As I left the office, I was glad that I had scheduled this appointment. The doctor was nice, compassionate, understanding, but he also seemed very thorough based on the questions he asked.

A sense of relief washed over me. I was glad I had taken the steps to schedule the appointment. I felt a renewed sense of hope. Finally, we were taking proactive steps towards uncovering the root of Jack's difficulties. Dr Dylan's warm demeanour and genuine concern for our son's well-being reassured me that we were in good hands. It was clear that he was not only a skilled professional, but also someone who genuinely cared about the people he worked with.

Finally, the day came for our appointment with Dr Dylan to discuss the outcome of Jack's assessment. I tried to make sense of my worries. I reminded myself that Jack's health and well-being was all that truly mattered. Still, I couldn't shake the apprehension that came with receiving a formal diagnosis.

Deep down, I knew that the diagnosis would come with the support and treatments Jack needed. It was time to face reality and stop holding onto the hope that he would eventually outgrow his challenges.

As we entered Dr Dylan's office, the tension in my chest eased slightly. He greeted us warmly and invited us to take a seat. "Let's talk about the results of Jack's assessment," Dr Dylan said, beginning the discussion that would shed some light on our son's challenges and provide us with some type of roadmap for the future. With a mix of anticipation and nervousness, we prepared ourselves to face whatever the evaluation revealed.

He handed us a copy of Jack's report. The pages were filled with detailed information, and I found myself attempting to absorb it all at once.

"Don't worry about reading it all, I will walk you through it," Dr Dylan said as he saw that I was trying to skim through the report and grasp the main points.

Taking a deep breath, I put aside the report and allowed myself to focus on what he was saying. He patiently explained each section of the report, breaking down the information into more manageable pieces.

"Jack's IQ is very high. He is a very intelligent kid." This took a bit of the edge off for me.

"Jack's working memory index is in the high average and his scores on his processing speed index are in the extremely high range," he added. "This suggests that he can hold his attention on tasks if he is interested in the topic. But his very high processing speed may explain some of his careless mistakes in school work. He is thinking much quicker than he can get the information down. Also, he may think he already knows what you are going to say as he has already processed it, so he may stop listening," he continued.

"However, his visual special index score is in the average range. Children with ADHD are known to have deficits in these abilities."

"What does that mean?" I asked.

"As Jack scored high on the working memory and processing speed, he still may find it challenging to retain relevant information and find it difficult to start and complete a task."

He then continued going through the report. "Another score in the very high range is fluid reasoning."

"What does that mean?" I asked.

"That he has excellent thinking and reasoning abilities. He can easily solve novel problems. This may also contribute to his defiance as he is well able to argue and negotiate." I smiled when he said it. That was so true.

"His verbal comprehension is average. He may struggle to find the words to communicate. This would also explain why he is reluctant to engage in reading and faces challenges with comprehension."

I took a deep breath as he paused.

"So, what does that mean now, does he have ADHD or not?" I asked, leaning forward in my chair.

"Jack shows many signs of ADHD, but his higher IQ complicates things. Gifted kids learn differently. They need to be more challenged."

"What should we do now that we know that he has ADHD?"

The doctor leaned forward in his seat. "There are a few options. Inform Jack's school of his diagnosis so they can help him manage his symptoms. Some considerations may include extra time to process instructions, give him more allowances for items being forgotten. At home, you can develop a more structured and organized routine. Create a schedule. Use checklists and visual reminders as they tend to be helpful. If this support isn't enough, medication is another option," he paused.

"Thanks," I said. "I hope these strategies work. I would rather not medicate him unless we really have to."

As I sat there, trying to process all of the information, Dr Dylan's empathetic gaze met mine. He took a deep breath before speaking. "This is a lot to digest," he acknowledged. "If you have any additional questions, don't hesitate to give me a call."

I couldn't wait to get home and read the report in more

detail and start implementing all the recommended strategies. But before that, I knew it was essential to sit down with Tom and Jack and discuss the results of the evaluation.

I tried my best to explain everything. I spoke about the strengths and challenges that were identified, emphasizing that the evaluation was meant to help us to support Jack better. Throughout the conversation, we made sure to reassure Jack that the diagnosis didn't define him.

We shared some of the strategies we would be exploring and I noticed a spark of excitement in Jack's eyes. Seeing that reaction was a significant victory for me.

The next day, I requested a meeting with Jack's Year Head teacher. It was important to inform her about the recent diagnosis and to seek the school's support. The meeting with her and the principal was scheduled in a couple of days. In the meantime, I shared the report with them, hoping it would provide them with additional insights.

As I walked into the principal's office, I knew that, this time, I was there to share an explanation for Jack's decreasing academic performance and his behaviour, and to outline potential solutions that could help us support him in a way that suited him best. They were both very understanding and compassionate. However, as I eagerly asked about the implementation of the doctor's recommended strategies, I was met with a response that left me feeling disheartened. "Each teacher has a considerable number of students to attend to, making it difficult to provide individual attention to Jack," said Mr McCarthy.

"We do have SEN, Special Education Needs teachers, but the number of resources is limited," added Ms Walsh.

I expressed my concerns about Jack's unique challenges and the importance of providing him with the right support. Seeing my disappointment and determination, Ms Walsh suggested, "We can move Jack's books to a library as there is always someone available, and they can help him make sure that he takes all the books he needs for his homework home." I appreciated the fact that they were trying, so I accepted the offer.

Jack tried this approach for a few days, but it made him feel different, excluded from his peers, so he requested to keep his books in the locker again. I understood—there is a lot of peer pressure in secondary school, and everyone is trying to fit in. He didn't want to be the one that stood out.

We implemented various strategies to support Jack. We created schedules and colour-coded them, which was a step towards promoting organization and structure in his daily life. The visual reminders proved to be effective to help him stay on track with his tasks and responsibilities.

For a while, it seemed like we were making progress. Again, I felt that glimmer of hope. However, I couldn't help but notice that these strategies had minimal impact on his behavioural issues. His impulsive outbursts and defiance persisted, leaving us feeling discouraged and unsure of how to address them effectively. We knew that there was a lot more to tackle and we were determined to find the right approach. With each setback, we were reminded of the complexities of Jack's condition. ADHD wasn't something that could be remedied with a quick fix—it required patience, understanding and consistent effort.

For the last couple of years, we had felt like we were living on a battlefield. Almost every interaction with Jack became a struggle and it was exhausting for all of us to be in constant survival mode. I realized that my reaction to every minor issue only added to the tension and stress. In an effort to preserve my own sanity, I made a conscious effort to choose my battles wisely.

Proudly Perplexed

I was well aware that disrespect and rebellion were common milestones of teenage development. I knew that Jack would likely argue with me, push for more independence and disagree with my decisions. I had mentally prepared myself for it. True to my expectations, Jack continued to test my boundaries, sought more privacy, expressed his frustrations with my parenting skills and regularly reminded me that I was ruining his life. There were times when he walked away from conversations in anger and slammed doors. He expressed these same feelings at school.

Jack's rebellious and disrespectful behaviour continued to impact his relationships with his teachers.

At this stage, I was convinced that the school principal and the Year Head had me on speed dial. His teachers clearly looked to us, as his parents, to improve the situation, and I have no doubt that they questioned our parenting skills and our discipline.

* * *

Life became a continuous cycle of arguments and tantrums, stretching from morning until night. Jack seemed to derive pleasure from deliberately provoking others, especially his parents and teachers. It appeared that he had no sense of when to stop, and he wasn't satisfied until he pushed someone to their limits. Ignoring his behaviour only fuelled his actions. The harder we tried to ignore it, the more he would keep pushing our buttons. And believe me when I say, he knew exactly what buttons to push.

You may still think that this is just typical teenage behaviour, however, most teenagers argue but will eventually give in. They may break rules, but they allow themselves to be grounded. When it came to our son, we lost control over him completely. In every argument, he would dig his heels in rather than yield. As soon as he felt threatened, it was on! Grounded? Please! Take computer time away? Please!

Once, we took his computer time away as a consequence of acting out. We explained the reasons and conditions for getting it back, hoping he would understand the impact of his actions. Surprisingly, Jack didn't protest or ask for his computer back for several days. I was so proud of him that he accepted the consequences so maturely.

Hold on! Something seems off... this doesn't sound like Jack. I decided to go and check on him in his room and see what he was up to. And what did I find? He was sitting there, fully engrossed in playing games on an Xbox. Xbox? We don't have Xbox. "Jack, where did you get that?" He had been hiding the Xbox for days and wasn't expecting me to catch him in the act.

"I borrowed it."

"Who did you borrow it from?"

He looked at me again, but this time, very annoyed. "Mom, you took my PC away, so I borrowed an Xbox from my friend." I had to step away for a moment as

I didn't know what else to say. I wasn't sure if I was supposed to be upset with him or proud of the creative way he managed to avoid the consequences.

Later that evening, while we were having dinner and chatting, I asked him again, "Who did you borrow the Xbox from?"

"Patrick," he blurted out. I knew Patrick was in his class and I had met his parents, so I just left it at that.

A couple of days later, I happened to run into Patrick's mom in a shopping centre. "Hi, how are you? I just wanted to say it was so kind of you and Patrick to lend Jack the Xbox."

She looked at me with a puzzled expression. "Xbox? We don't have an Xbox. Our kids are not allowed to use computers or the Xbox." I could only stand and stare at her with a blank face, ashamed and speechless. "Oh, maybe I misunderstood. It must have been someone else in Jack's class."

As soon as I got home, I approached Jack and asked him who he had borrowed the Xbox from. "Patrick," he responded agitatedly.

"Patrick from your class?"

"Yes!"

"And there is only one Patrick in your class, correct?"

"Yes!"

"Hmmm, I just met Patrick's mom in the shopping centre and thanked her for lending you Patrick's Xbox."

He looked up at me, his eyes wide with surprise. "You did what?! Why did you do that, Mom?"

"Jack, would you like to tell me where you got the Xbox from?"

"No!" and he walked away.

I approached this conversation again a few minutes later. "Jack, where did you get the Xbox? There won't be any consequences if you tell me the truth."

"Ok," he responded with a quiet and soft voice. "I bought it." I tried to stay calm even though I felt the blood rushing to my head.

"Where did you get the money from?"

"I took it from Daddy's bag." So, he stole the money.

"Stay calm, stay calm," I kept reminding myself. "Where did you buy it?"

"Online, and then I went to pick it up a few days back." That was another thing that concerned me. So, instead of getting angry, I decided to discuss online safety with him and all the possible things that could have gone wrong. "How do you think Dad will feel when you tell him that you took money he has worked hard for without his permission?" I saw that I had gone too far.

He got agitated. "I don't care!" he shouted and left.

Magic Pill?

The efforts we made so far hadn't resulted in the improvements we had hoped for, and the challenges persisted as Jack reached the middle of his second year. The possibility of resorting to ADHD medication weighed heavily on my mind. While I understood that medication could potentially help manage some of Jack's behaviours, I was still hesitant and cautious about taking that next step.

I approached our family doctor to gather more information about ADHD medication. We learned that only psychiatrists were authorized to prescribe the medication in Ireland. He helped me fill out the application form that needed to be sent to the Child and Adolescent Mental Health Services organization in order to find a psychiatrist. On my way home, I posted it with the hope that someone would contact us soon so we could continue exploring our options.

I won't forget the response of some of my family members when they found out about the diagnosis and our treatment approach. "Why do you want to drug your child?" they asked. That was a question I struggled with myself. Was medication the right choice? Would the medication harm him? Affect him in a negative way? Would it have a long-term impact? Would he be the same child?

In the meantime, I leaned on my friends and shared my troubles with them. I joined a gym just to get away from my problems. I continued to read books and internet articles about ADHD. I joined ADHD Parent Support Facebook groups, which were comforting. They understood what I was going through and validated my efforts as a parent. Some of them also recommended that I consider putting Jack on medication as it was a standard ADHD treatment. They shared their stories with me and I noticed that many of the children were on and off medication. Some improved dramatically. They were able to sit still at school. They were much calmer and able to hold a conversation without getting constantly irritated. Medication didn't erase all the symptoms of ADHD as they were still a bit fidgety, but it helped reduce the symptoms.

It was four months before the end of his second year and we still hadn't heard back from the Child Mental Health Services.

I started my search for a private psychiatrist in our area. I made numerous phone calls only to be met with the same response, "There is a very long waiting list. It will take a couple of years before we get to you." Or, "I am sorry, but we have closed our waiting list as it was too long and we are not taking any new patients at the moment."

Determined to find the support Jack needed, I stumbled upon an online company that offered psychiatrist services and virtual consultations.

They had a child psychiatrist who specialised in ADHD, Dr Ahmed.

Dr Ahmed requested a copy of Jack's evaluation form from the psychologist. He also asked Jack's teachers to complete an ADHD questionnaire. Luckily, we had already done that for the psychologist.

During the initial online meeting, Dr Ahmed reviewed Jack's results. He confirmed the initial diagnosis of ADHD and recommended that Jack start on a small dose of Straterra. Based on my research, Straterra was one of the non-stimulant medications used to treat ADHD symptoms. For some children with ADHD, non-stimulant medications were not effective, but it felt like a good option to start with. Non-stimulant medication had been shown to improve overall concentration and impulse control. We agreed that we would meet every four weeks to monitor the impact of the medication on Jack and discuss any side effects. I liked the fact that he wanted Jack to be closely monitored and we agreed that we would adjust the dose as needed. He also asked us to contact our family doctor and get Jack's blood pressure, height and weight measured. He wanted to make sure that everything was in order before he started his meds.

When we met with our family doctor, his response was unexpected. He was shocked when I explained that we were working with an online doctor to prescribe Straterra to Jack. "You went to an online doctor? Who is that doctor? Is he even certified to practice medicine? That can be very dangerous!" he said and seemed very upset with me. While I agreed with him, I also reassured him that I had checked the doctor's credentials. My reassurances seemed to sway him but he was not completely convinced. "This is not how we do things here. We are not used to working with online doctors. We need to wait for the referral to be accepted."

I leaned forward in my seat, and with a firm voice, responded, "While I understand your concerns, I have done all my due diligence and checked the doctor's credentials. We submitted the referral form over six months ago and we still haven't heard back. Jack needs help and I am not willing to wait any longer and watch him struggle. So, I am doing the best I can with the support that is available to me. I hope you can understand."

He finally accepted my explanation and fetched the blood pressure monitor. "I understand, there are waiting lists everywhere. I know that you want the best for Jack, this is just not how we are used to doing things here."

I sent all the relevant information via email to Dr

Ahmed, and a couple of hours later, he sent me a prescription for Jack's medication.

* * *

Not even a week had passed since Jack started on the medication and we could already see some improvements. He was sitting still rather than hanging upside down on his chair and was able to engage in conversations. He was more present in class. It was also encouraging that there hadn't been any serious side effects so far. Even his teachers were noticing improvements. It was the first time we had received positive feedback from Jack's Year Head.

When we met with Dr Ahmed to discuss the effects of the medication, he was very pleased. "That's excellent! It is great to see that Jack is responding to this medication so well. For many children, it takes up to four months to start seeing benefits." He also added that some of the behavioural problems Jack was experiencing wouldn't go away with medication alone and he recommended seeking help from a behavioural therapist. We decided to keep him on the lower dose of Straterra and continue to check in every four weeks.

* * *

"Mom, I don't feel good," Jack announced one morning after taking his medication. "I don't like the medication. It doesn't make me feel good."

"Really?" I asked, trying to stay calm.

"Yeah, I don't feel good."

I asked him to eat something and drink some water. He felt much better. So, we made sure that he never took the medication on an empty stomach. There were days when he felt good on the medication and days when he complained about not feeling good. I discussed this with Dr Ahmed during our next appointment. "Jack has been on this medication for two months now. If he was experiencing side effects, he wouldn't just experience them on certain days. Could there be another reason behind it? Maybe he doesn't want to take the medication?"

I kept an eye on Jack over the next few days, especially when I gave him his morning dose. I noticed that when he took the pill, he would immediately run to the bathroom. I realised that he was spitting out his meds. The next day, he walked away with the pill in his hand. So, I followed him quietly. He was next to my yoga mat, which made me wonder what he was doing there. As soon as he walked away, I checked under the yoga mat and found a few pills hidden there. He wasn't taking his medication regularly, which I believe was causing some of his side effects.

Discussing this with Jack, it became clear that he was against taking medication. "Mom, the pills don't make me feel good, I don't want to take them."

I said, "We can discuss this with Dr Ahmed. Maybe he can prescribe a different medication for you. Look at all the benefits we have seen over the past couple of months," and I started listing out all the improvements. "No, I don't want any medication!"

There was no way of convincing him otherwise. He wanted to feel 'normal', so he didn't want to do or take anything that made him feel different. Medication was a physical manifestation of the differences between him and his friends—it was 'proof' that there was something 'wrong' with him. He found being different so painful and so unacceptable that he was in denial about his problems, even when there was a price to pay.

We pleaded with him to take the medication, convinced that it would maximize his potential. It was heartbreaking to watch him struggle in school and we were worried about the consequences these years would have on his future as an adult. In the end, forcing or tricking him into taking the medication wasn't an option. The ultimate decision regarding the medication was his. Once again, we were back to square one.

Short-Lived Therapy

Exploring behavioural therapy, as Dr Ahmed recommended, seemed like a promising avenue. However, finding a behavioural therapist who specialised in working with children and had experience with ADHD proved to be a difficult task. There were two options—wait for the Child Mental Health Services to get back to us or go private. Unfortunately, we couldn't find even private therapists specializing in children with ADHD in our region. The closest available option would have required a three-hour drive each way for a weekly therapy session, which was simply not feasible.

In the end, we found an occupational therapist who worked with children and had plenty of experience working with children with ADHD. After our initial meeting, we agreed that the best first step would be to explore emotions with Jack. Is he able to recognize and name emotions in others? Is he able to recognize and name emotions in himself?

His first OT session was approaching and I was worried that he would refuse to go, but to my surprise, he got ready that morning and off we went. As we were driving, he asked, "Mom, do I have to?"

"Why don't you give it a try, Jack? You may actually like the therapist. If this doesn't help or doesn't work, we can discuss other options."

"Ok," he responded, not sounding very convinced.

After the first three sessions, Jack came away with a lot of knowledge about emotions, including the blue, green, yellow and red zones of emotions. On the way home, we would play games where he would try to act out an emotion in each zone.

After the session, the therapist and I would have a small chat about how the session went and what I could do at home to support him. But the more I spoke to her about ADHD symptoms and asked questions, the more I realized that I seemed to have more knowledge than she did.

After the therapy office was closed for a week, we faced some challenges trying to get Jack back to his session. The break from therapy seemed to have disrupted his routine and made it difficult for him to readjust. "I don't want to go. I don't care about the consequences. I am not going! End of discussion!" Jack responded.

I knew that forcing him would only result in a heated argument, which could then escalate into a tantrum, but ultimately wouldn't change his mind. So, I agreed that we wouldn't go. That was the end of occupational therapy for us.

Dispatching the Parent Police

As the days and months went by, I braced myself for what I thought would be an ongoing battle of frequent tantrums.

Tantrums that always started with begging and with

the familiar sentence, "Mom, please! Mom, I beg you! Mom, please!"

"Here comes another one," I would think. And when I was unable to cope anymore and attempted to take a short walk just to calm myself down, he would follow me out into the street. Barefoot, screaming, yelling, and crying for everyone to see. "Please stop, Jack! Everyone can see and hear you," I would beg.

"No! Mom, please! Mom, I beg you! Mom, please!"

He was hoping that I would get embarrassed and give him what he wanted.

He would throw tantrums at home and open the windows. Living in an estate, our neighbours are close by, so they could hear everything. Jack was well aware of this, so he would start screaming for help, "Help! Please, help me!" just to get attention from the neighbours or people walking by in the hopes that I would give in. To be honest, I often did give in. I wasn't able to handle it. I just couldn't cope.

Stealing money sadly became a regular occurrence. It was disheartening to see Jack repeatedly resorting to such behaviour as it not only affected our trust in him, but also created a tense atmosphere at home. The amount of money he took escalated from small sums to more significant ones, totalling hundreds of euros. He was resourceful at finding ways to access cash, going so far as to search through our bags and purses to find money he could use for online gaming or a new phone he wanted.

When we discovered he had purchased a new phone using money he took from Tom's bag, we decided to confiscate it. We hoped that it would help him understand that he shouldn't take what didn't belong to him without permission as our regular conversations were not helping.

Jack saw that arguing with us would not get him his new phone back, so he went upstairs and locked himself in his room.

We agreed to give him some space to cool off when the doorbell rang unexpectedly.

"Who could it be at this hour? It is well past 10," I asked my husband, my heart racing in sync with the gloomy toll of the doorbell.

I opened the door and a pair of policemen emerged from the shadows. "We were called here because of a domestic dispute."

My jaw dropped in disbelief. "What domestic dispute?" I asked, looking very confused.

"May we come in?" one of the officers asked.

Reluctantly, I invited them inside and showed them to our living room.

As they walked in, my husband jumped out of his seat, "What is going on?" he asked.

"We have received a phone call from Jack concerning the confiscation of his phone. He appeared deeply distressed, so we were compelled to investigate and ensure that everything is ok here," one of the officers explained.

"Jack called you?" I stammered, not knowing what else to say.

I took a deep breath and explained, "Jack is our 14-year-old son. We took his phone away as a consequence of his actions."

"May we speak with Jack?" the officer asked firmly. I stood there feeling embarrassed, wishing for the earth to swallow me up. Then I heard my husband calling for Jack. "Jack, can you please come down, there are two police officers here that would like to talk to you."

Jack walked into the living room, his head held high, his shoulders back, looking very proud of himself. He assumed that we would be the ones reprimanded.

To his surprise, things turned out quite differently. The officers took the time to talk to him, explaining that we, as his parents, are the authority figures in the house and we are the ones who make and reinforce the rules.

Jack just stood there, not saying a word. It was obviously not how he envisioned the conversation going.

I apologized to the police officers for the inconvenience caused and showed them to the door. But Jack recovered from this setback almost immediately. As soon as the door was closed, he began asking for his phone, which escalated into a tantrum of great intensity.

Shadows of Suffering

I still believed that consequences were the correct way to discipline Jack and influence his behaviour. But no matter what approach I took, it always seemed to backfire.

Each time I stepped out of the house, he would lock me out, leaving me stranded in our back garden. I lost count of how many times I found myself sitting there, crying in the cold and rain after he refused to let me in. It was one of the many 'resourceful' ways he used to try to manipulate me into giving in to his demands. In those moments, I felt utterly desperate, lost and filled with pain. I no longer recognized my own child, and I no longer recognized myself. Coping became an impossible task and I felt a mix of shame and fear at the overwhelming feelings I had. As I sat there, I caught myself disliking my own child, yearning for someone to come and take him away, to provide me with some relief. I even found myself contemplating packing my bags and leaving just to escape it all. I wished in those moments that he was never born.

What would my life look like if he wasn't there? How can I dislike my own flesh and blood... my baby? The guilt of feeling this way weighed heavily on me, but it was born from a deep desire to flee from the daily struggle. Despite these feelings, I knew that I would never actually leave—it was just a fantasy born out of exhaustion and despair. The day-in and day-out battles were wearing me down. They changed me and they changed our family.

I was convinced that I couldn't handle my child's ADHD, and self-pity became my worst enemy. I felt miserable, drained, and utterly alone in the world. Nobody could help me. I was consumed by negative thoughts, ruminating and feeling even more sorry for myself. I found myself trapped in a never-ending pity party.

I doubted myself and felt the weight of judgment from within and the outside world. I was beyond weary from crying myself to sleep—on the nights I managed to sleep at all.

Despite the urge to give up, I knew I needed to pull myself together. Giving up simply wasn't an option. With the last bit of strength I could muster, I kept repeating to myself, "If I am ok, Jack will be ok. He needs me and he is worth it." That gave me the determination to continue with the hope that something would somehow change.

And it did. It got even worse! The tantrums persisted and took an unexpected turn, becoming physical. When everything he tried seemed ineffective, he would resort to squeezing my hand and punching me. In those moments, I looked into his eyes and it was like gazing at a stranger. The level of rage I could see in him frightened me. I wasn't sure what he was capable of. I felt as though he was standing on the edge of a cliff and no words could bring him back. He needed a way to calm himself down, but he didn't know how. "Jack, you are hurting me, please stop," I begged while tears were rolling down my cheeks. However, he just took my response as confirmation that what he was doing was working. Whenever I tried to walk away, he would follow me, gripping my arm tightly.

Consumed by fear, I found myself giving in to his demands. When he finally got what he wanted, he would break down into tears. I would hold him close as he cried himself to sleep. He was emotionally wrecked. His rage and anger seemed to consume him completely, leaving him unable to regulate the intensity of his emotions. My heart ached for him as I held him in my arms.

When children throw a tantrum or have a meltdown, what helps is to hold them in your arms and let them calm down. Reassure them that you are there for them and that you love them. For Jack, it was different.

A tantrum could kick off at any time. One evening, he refused to go to bed. He wanted to play on his computer with his friends, who were unfortunately still up playing on their computers at that hour. I explained to him that it was late and he needed rest, but he wasn't having any of it. The tantrum started with him stomping his feet and yelling, then it quickly escalated. He was in full meltdown mode. "Mom, please! Mom, I beg you! Mom, please!" I could feel the tension in the air as Tom and I exchanged worried glances. We were in for a long night.

Jack's persistence was wearing us down, but we knew we couldn't give in. It was a battle of wills and we were determined to stand our ground. As Jack continued to plead and scream, I could see the frustration building up inside him. He was like a volcano about to erupt. I knew that one wrong move could set him off and I was afraid what might happen next. Tom gently tried to reason with him, but it was like talking to a brick wall. Jack was in a state where no amount of rationality could reach him.

Around midnight, Tom and I decided not to engage with Jack's tantrum and hoped that he would eventually tire himself out and go to bed. Fat Chance. He persisted, following us into our bedroom, pleading and begging. "Mom, please! Mom, I beg you! Mom, please!"

Tom asked him nicely to go to bed, promising to discuss it all in the morning. We knew that there was no point in reasoning with him.

Instead, Jack resorted to his old strategy and opened a window in the hallway to try and attract the attention of our neighbours "Help! I need help! Help, please!" He kept screaming out of the windows, unconcerned about how disruptive this was to others who were trying to sleep.

"Jack, please stop, you will wake up the neighbours," my husband asked him politely.

"Good!" Jack responded and continued screaming out of the window. After a few minutes, he noticed that we were not reacting to it, so he came back to our bed. "Mom, please! Mom, I beg you! Mom, please!"

It was past midnight and Tom and I were both helpless with no idea how to break through to him. In a desperate attempt to de-escalate the situation, Tom carried Jack to his room and sat on the bed and held him in his arms. But Jack's rage only intensified, kicking, screaming, and hitting while Tom tried to hold him.

I looked at Tom's face and I could see the pain and desperation in his eyes. Then I noticed the blood running down his face. Jack had accidentally kicked him, cutting him across the eye.

"Please stop!" I yelled.

"All of us will now go to bed and this will be discussed in the morning." We were all so emotionally drained at this stage—even Jack agreed to call it a night.

Lying there, replaying these events in my mind, I couldn't fall asleep.

When I looked at the clock, it was 3 am. Tom was lying next to me, but I knew he was also awake. "You can't sleep either?" I asked.

He turned around, looked at me and said, "No."

I sighed, "I was thinking about what happened. Looking at you holding Jack, I saw a dad who wanted to help his child, who wanted to hold him and protect him as he was going through this emotional turmoil. In your efforts, all I saw was the best of intentions and love. But when I looked at Jack, it was like looking at an animal in a cage, fighting to break free. It was like he had forgotten who you were. His instincts were telling him to fight and get out of your grasp."

My husband kept looking at me and I could see that he was trying to process what I had just said. "Hmm," was all he said before he turned around and fell asleep. I did my best to follow suit. The next morning, Jack woke up like nothing had happened, completely oblivious to the chaos he caused the night before. But Tom's face bore evidence of the struggle. I winced when I saw the cut above his eye, which had also swollen during the few hours of sleep that he got. We knew that we needed to tell Jack that hitting and kicking, or otherwise hurting anyone was not ok. But we also recognized that he wasn't fully in control of his actions during those intense episodes.

The next morning, I made another appointment with our family doctor as we still hadn't heard from the Child Mental Health Services and I was desperate. The doctor empathised with me but couldn't offer any other options. "They have a long waiting list, but we can submit another referral." So, we submitted another referral, and the waiting continued.

School Dropout Manifesto

Jack kept complaining that school was boring, and each morning, it became more and more difficult for us to convince him to go. Then, one morning, he just decided he wouldn't go. We woke up and heard Jack in the shower so we knew he was awake. He got dressed, had his breakfast and was ready to leave. I watched him from the kitchen putting on his shoes and opening the front door. "Bye, have a good day at school!" I called out from the kitchen. I heard the door closing. I took a deep breath... finally, I could make myself a coffee, sit down and relax for a few minutes before work.

Wait, what was that noise? There's someone in the house! I walked out of the kitchen and was surprised to see Jack sitting at the top of the stairs. "Is everything ok? Did something happen?"

"Yeah."

"Why aren't you going to school?"

"I don't want to."

"Why? Did something happen at school?"

"No, I just don't want to go."

"Jack, can you please go to school, you're going to be late. We can talk about it when you get home."

"No, I am not going."

I sat down next to him to have a conversation with him. "Is everything ok?"

"Yes, I am just not going to school."

I even offered to write him a late note and drop him off at school, but he refused. "No, I am not going!" And every time I tried to convince him, his response kept getting firmer and louder, "I said I am not going!" until he got up and went to his room.

I followed him, at this point very agitated and worried. "Jack, please go to school!" I yelled.

He yelled back through his closed bedroom door, "No, I am not going! How many times do I need to tell you that I am not going!"

"Jack, how am I going to explain this to your teachers? Can you please just go to school!"

"Leave me alone! I said I am not going!"

"Ok, if you are not going, just so we are clear, you are not going to be allowed to sit there and play on your computer or phone the whole day!"

"Fine, but I am still not going!"

He was 14... I couldn't just take him into my arms and load him into the car. With that, the conversation ended.

The following day, he decided to go to school. I tried to find out if there was an underlying reason why he had refused the day before but could get nothing out of him.

The next morning, I woke up to a text message. I checked my phone and there was a message from Jack. "Mom, I am not going to school today. I understand the consequences. My computer is off, my phone is in the kitchen. I love you."

Was this a joke? Is he really not going to school again? I came running out of my room and found him still in his bedroom. "Mom, I said I am not going to school, so leave me alone!"

Feeling utterly powerless, I went downstairs and made myself a cup of coffee. I sat down at the kitchen table and started considering my options. There was only one option really at this stage—just let him be.

Later that day, he came down for lunch like it was his day off. "Jack, you made a choice not to go to school today. I won't be lying to your teachers that you were not feeling well. I will tell them."

He shrugged, "Ok, I don't care!" He ate his lunch and brought me down his school journal so I could write the note.

I opened the journal and stared at the empty page for a few minutes. Should I cover for him and lie? What was the right thing to do? He needed to learn that he was responsible and accountable for his choices. I wouldn't lie. So, I wrote, "Jack hasn't been at school today as he made the decision not to go. I don't have an explanation for his choice at this stage. I will accept and support any consequences you may see fitting for his absence."

The following morning, I woke up to a text again. I prayed before I even looked at it that it wasn't from Jack. But what would be the chances? Of course it was a text from Jack. This was starting to feel like Groundhog Day.

Since what I was doing wasn't working, I thought maybe bribing him would.

That afternoon, we sat down and asked him if he would

like to have his computer and phone back. "Yes, please!" he responded enthusiastically. "Ok, you will get it every day you go to school and over the weekend. If you don't go to school, they will be taken away from you."

"Deal!"

To my surprise, the next morning, I woke up to a running shower. "He is getting ready for school," I thought to myself. "Ok, but don't get too excited. Until he closes the door and actually leaves the house, nothing is guaranteed."

I was sitting on the edge of my chair in the kitchen, watching every step he took. I was breathing as quietly as possible, not saying anything, so as not to upset him. I was so worried he would change his mind. Then I heard the door closing. He was outside the house. I ran towards the window to watch him walk to school. What a relief, he went to school! That was a win for us and I would take every win I could get at this stage.

Over the next few days, Jack left every morning and came home as soon as school finished. He spent most of his time in his room doing his homework and on the phone with his friends. All was good again in our house.

Until... a few days later, my phone rang midmorning. I put the dishes down and dried my hands to answer. Jack's school name was on the caller ID.

Shit. I forced myself to pick up.

"Hello, this is Ms Walsh, can we talk?"

"Of course, is everything ok?" I answered, my heart was pounding.

"I was just wondering if everything is ok with Jack. He hasn't been in school for the past few days."

"No, that is not possible. He was at school all last week and I saw him leave the house only a few hours ago. You must be mistaken."

"I checked the attendance report and he has been marked absent every day of last week and today."

"Is there a chance that he was late and the teachers forgot to update the attendance report?" As soon as I said it, I knew that wasn't the case.

"That can't be. Every teacher takes attendance at the beginning of their class. Let me quickly check the class he is supposed to be in now and I will call you back in a few minutes."

"Thank you, that would be much appreciated!"

I knew that if I continued to believe that Jack was actually going to school and that he was sitting in the class today, I would be lying to myself. But, just this once, I kept hoping I was wrong.

I paced around the kitchen, waiting for Ms Walsh to call me back.

Finally! The phone rang.

"Hello? Did you find him?"

"I am sorry, but he is not in his class. I even checked the principal's office and bathrooms, but Jack is not here."

My face was turning red—I wasn't sure if it was from the anger or the embarrassment that I had no clue where my child was.

"Thank you! I will drive around and see if I can find him. I will call you as soon as I do."

The minute I hung up the phone, I got into my car and started driving around. I wasn't exactly sure where to even start looking. I started in our estate, then moved onto the main street. As I was coming down the street next to Jack's school, I saw him walking on the footpath. He didn't see me as I drove towards him—not until the car was beside him. Then he finally noticed me and his face said it all. He knew that he had been caught and was in trouble. I opened the passenger door and he got in. I said nothing. I started driving towards the school with the intention of dropping him off. "I am not going to school! If you take me to school, I will get out of the car and run! I am not going to school!" Jack yelled. So, I drove us home.

There were still another two weeks of school left. Was there anything I could do to convince him to go?

I reached out to parent support groups and other family support groups for advice. Everyone told me to find out if there was something else going on that I wasn't aware of that could be causing him distress at school like bullying, fear of exams, or fights with friends. But I wasn't able to identify any other underlying reason behind the refusal, except that he found school boring.

So, I approached the school directly and asked for help.

Once again, I found myself sitting in the principal's office. Mr McCarthy and Ms Walsh were very helpful. They came up with different suggestions as we explored what Jack didn't like about school. They agreed that he didn't have to wear a uniform until the end of the school year as that was one thing I knew Jack disliked. We even agreed on days during the week when he could start school late or finish early by skipping some of the non-exam classes. We presented the plan to Jack and he agreed to it.

I was happy with the outcome of this meeting, thinking that the next day would be easier. Oh, how wrong I was. "I am not going to school today!" was the first thing I heard when I opened my eyes.

I asked the school to discuss our situation with the education welfare officer who visited the school regularly as I didn't know where else to turn to for help.

As the school year was almost over, all they could do was file a report and see how the next school year went.

When I asked Jack what he would like to be when he grows up, his response was, "A school dropout." He didn't want to hear about financial difficulties, about difficulties finding a job in the future… he just wanted to drop out of school. He even googled all the laws and information, and every time I brought up the topic of school, he would recite the legal precedent or statute back to me. I lost count of the number of times I heard that the minimum school leaving age was 16, or until students had completed three years of second-level education—whichever was later. For him, that meant another year of school and his 'dream' would come true—he could finally drop out. He couldn't wait.

Jack spent the remaining two weeks of the school year at home, in his room, without his computer or phone. I went to check on him a few times and I was met with a terse, "Leave me alone!" While I am not entirely sure what he was doing that time, on those occasions, I found him lying on his bed, lost in music, with his legs propped against the wall and occasionally tossing a small ball against it. He came down from his room a few times during the day, expressing how bored he was. I felt very conflicted. I knew that arguing and forcing wouldn't get us anywhere, but not doing anything felt like I was condoning his choices. So, from time to time, I reminded him that I was not ok with this and that he should reconsider this decision. As a parent, I struggled to find the right balance between compassion for his situation and determination to get him to do the right thing. I cared about Jack's feelings, but I knew I had to stay strong. I needed to keep his future in mind. Life was hard enough for him with ADHD... I didn't want him to fall further behind by neglecting his education.

PART 4
PUTTING THE PUZZLE TOGETHER

Taking the Reins

The worries of a mother never stop. As we finally made it to the summer holidays, I knew I had to use this brief period to figure things out before the new school year began.

Being helpless is one thing, but accepting it and just giving up, resigning myself to defeat, was not an option I even considered. So, I made a conscious decision that the changes should start with me.

I decided to learn more about ADHD on my own. If nobody else out there could help me understand my child and support my family, I would do it alone. I devoured every parenting book I could get my hands on—books about child development, ADHD... anything that might provide a hint on a better way to manage Jack. But no matter what we tried, he resisted every attempt to improve the situation.

The more I read, the more questions I had and the more I reflected on the past few years. I realized that I had been focusing on what this was like for me and my husband, and not once did I stop to think of things from Jack's point of view. What was this like for Jack? What was going through his head to cause this? He was not a bad person—far from it. I realised I needed to separate who he was from how he behaved and acted. I was focusing on the symptoms instead of trying to understand the root cause. When a flower doesn't bloom, we first look to fix problems in the environment in which it grows. We don't just write off the flower as being broken or defective. So, why am I trying to fix my child? Is my child broken? Or is his school and home environment not suitable for him? Isn't that something that we should be looking at first?

* * *

My research led me to ADHD training and I decided to learn more about how the ADHD brain works. What is so unique about it? What environment does someone with ADHD need to thrive? Is it exclusive to every individual? Will that environment need to change as the child grows into an adult? The knowledge I gained was profound. It helped me understand my child and get to know the real him. It completely changed my interactions with him and helped me accept him for who he is. I now have newly found compassion for him and have learned to love him again. I have realised that love is a choice, and I made the choice to love my child and raise him as best as I know how, understanding that I can't avoid the inevitable pain that comes with it.

As knowledge is power, here are some things that I have learned that I wanted to share with you all, to empower you to get to know and understand your child—or even yourself if you have been diagnosed with ADHD—just a little bit more.

One thing I want to point out is that ADHD is unique to each person and can show up differently from situation to situation. There are different types of ADHD and not everyone who has it is hyper. Some people with inattentive type ADHD may be seen as the most mellow person in the group!

The examples I am sharing are specific to the experience we had. I hope they can serve as a guide and help you to ignite your own curiosity about the bright and gifted ADHD brain.

Uniquely Wired Brain

Let's Imagine the ADHD brain as a custom-built sports car, each one uniquely designed and wired for high performance. But unlike the standard models, these cars come with their own set of controls, buttons and switches. Now, if we are not aware of the custom features and simply drive it as if it was a regular car, we will struggle with the unfamiliar controls. It would be like trying to navigate a rocket ship with a bicycle manual. But when we take time to understand the intricacies of this extraordinary machine, we will unlock its full potential, and it can outperform even most standard vehicles on the road.

Understanding the wiring of the ADHD brain is like getting the owner's manual for the sports car. It allows us to tailor our approach, fine-tune the engine, and navigate the fast lanes of life in a way that complements its unique design. We will be able to embrace the exceptional features that come with this one-of-a-kind vehicle.

Moreover, the sports car comes with the ability to upgrade and rewire its internal systems. It's like installing a high-speed internet connection in a vehicle—with practice, the ADHD brain can rewire itself to improve memory, attention and focus. Just as a skilled mechanic can fine-tune the engine of its unique vehicle, individuals with ADHD can develop strategies and techniques to optimize their brain's performance.

The brain's ability to reorganize itself by forming new neural pathways is called neuroplasticity.

If we practice gratitude, positive self-talk, focus on

memories and our strengths, our brain can make more neural connections and rewire.

Now, let's consider the environment this sports car operates in. It is essential to provide the right track, one where its unique features can shine. By tailoring the environment to suit the sports car specifications, we can ensure that it performs at its best and achieves remarkable feats on its own terms, just as the ADHD brain will excel in the right environment.

One year, Jack's class was working on delivering a Christmas Carol concert for friends and family. Not only did they have to practice a lot, but the room had to be decorated, the stage needed to be set up, along with numerous other tasks. Jack not only participated, but he also helped the teachers and his classmates come up with solutions that addressed certain problems and saved valuable time. Teachers were praising him for his organizational and problem-solving skills. They were impressed by his level of energy, enthusiasm and passion for ensuring that everything ran as smoothly as possible and everyone had a great experience.

But after the Christmas break, we were called into school again as Jack was disturbing the class by being too enthusiastic, not being able to sit quietly, and constantly talking and disturbing others. And the question they asked was, "Where is the Jack who was helping us organize the Christmas Carol concert?

Why is he not able to demonstrate the same level of commitment and respect in the classroom?"

The interesting thing is that the qualities he demonstrated in the classroom and in helping to organize the Christmas Carol concert had not changed. However, because the environment was different, suddenly what people valued as strengths became weaknesses and weren't appreciated at all.

This taught me that the environment plays a key role in ensuring someone thrives, flourishes and is an asset instead of withering and becoming a difficulty that needs to be managed.

Epiphany: Cracking the Code

Developmental Delay

Children with a bright and gifted ADHD brain experience developmental delays and mature later than their peers. In many cases, the delay can be anywhere from three to six years. What an eye-opener for us! It explained Jack's emotional immaturity compared to his peers—his inability to articulate what he was feeling and what he was going through. This had nothing to do with me going back to work too early, Jack becoming too independent at a young age or our parenting skills.

It also had nothing to do with his intelligence or capabilities.

However, we couldn't ignore this developmental delay when thinking about his future. He might need support from his parents a bit longer, might not be ready to go straight to college or to work after he finishes school (I still have hopes that he will finish secondary school). If work or college aren't good options, other plans will need to be put in place to support him and help him grow into a young, confident adult who will be able to enjoy life to its fullest.

Executive Functions

I believe it is important to look at the concept of executive functions before we continue to explore other areas. Executive function is an umbrella term for the management system of the brain. Executive functioning skills are housed in the part of the brain that is responsible for overseeing all other brain functions—like an air traffic control system at a busy airport managing arrivals and departures.

Executive functions can be used to identify and explain many of the cognitive challenges people with ADHD tend to struggle with.

The symptoms of a weak executive function aligned with many of the struggles that Jack faced on a daily basis, including not being able to sustain attention, being distracted, losing his books at school, forgetting his homework, the messy room, the poor personal hygiene, being unable to regulate emotions, and even getting lost in the house on his way from the living room into the kitchen. The good news was that, with help and support, he could strengthen his executive functioning skills.

Performance Inconsistency and Interest

The bright and gifted ADHD brain is wired to seek out interest rather than importance or priority. It doesn't matter how important something is to others, if the ADHD brain doesn't find it interesting, it won't be able to pay attention. It doesn't mean that people with ADHD don't love or care about that person, it is just the way their brain works.

Interest is the fuel that stimulates our brain. Our brains cannot focus or work without interest, in the same way a car won't get going without fuel, no matter how good the engine is. Interest can be positive or negative, so even crises and drama can be interesting to us.

People with ADHD cannot pay attention to something if it doesn't interest them.

This went a long way to explain Jack's inconsistent performances not only in different subjects, but also in different topics within a given subject. Teachers used to say to us, "Last week, he was so engaged and did so well in his test. What changed?" Or, "He is not motivated but we know that he is capable, he just needs to put more effort in." At the time, we couldn't answer that question and didn't understand the reason why. Now we know that the topic itself or the way it was taught that week was of interest to him, so he was able to focus on it fully but then couldn't focus on other topics he found boring. His interest dictated his ability to focus. It was not just his natural interest in the subject or activity that was important. If he was anticipating something fun, or when something unexpected happened, this could also spark his interest.

From our conversations and observing his actions, I can confirm that he is unable to sustain even minimal focus or be engaged fully in a topic that he doesn't find interesting. In certain situations, he was seen as very bright and capable, and in others as a poor performer, lacking motivation and even a bit lazy.

And if I am being honest with myself and all of you, that wasn't just an opinion held by his teachers. Even we as parents saw him the same way many times.

However, now we have learned to differentiate between the times when he **won't** do something vs. when he **can't** do something because of the way his brain is wired. That has allowed us to have more compassionate conversations with him and support him in a way we couldn't before. It has changed the stories we told ourselves, and others, about our son.

Entertain or Engage Me!

Everyone feels bored now and again. But most of us can complete a task even when we find it boring. I lost count of the number of times I had to complete an expense report, but I can easily remember how many times I enjoyed it... zero!

But for someone with ADHD, trying to complete a task they find uninteresting can seem a near-impossible challenge. The bright and gifted ADHD brain simply must be engaged or entertained. This can be a source of drama or trouble as they will seek entertainment even if it is at the expense of another person.

It cannot stand being bored. Boredom—that restless, intense feeling—can be almost painful. Boredom to ADHD is like kryptonite to Superman. Boredom can arise at home, at an event, at school, on holidays, and while watching TV. The ADHD brain can get bored anywhere and at any time.

Jack always said that school was boring. We thought it was just a phase. He would be bored when we went for a walk or for a swim on the beach. He would be bored when we were in the cinema watching a movie he had picked! I couldn't understand it. How could he be bored in the middle of doing something he asked to do? Something he was actively participating in? Boredom at this level is very hard to explain to others, especially when they are having a great time.

Waiting for his turn at amusement parks, standing in the queue at a shopping centre, at football training... it was all painfully boring for him. His brain needed to be constantly engaged. And that didn't always mean engaging in positive and meaningful experiences and activities. Boredom led him to say things or act in a certain way that he probably regretted later. He would start arguments for the sake of starting arguments, he would annoy people and push their buttons to get a reaction out of them, disrupt the entire class when he felt there wasn't anything interesting to do. All just to avoid boredom. His brain could not bear to be bored. Now I understand how uncomfortable those experiences must have been for him. I say I understand, but I'll never fully get it as I will never experience the world the way he does.

Many of the chores and banal things that he had to do at home, he considered boring. So, as soon as I asked him to clean his room, his brain would flag it as a boring thing before he even had the chance to begin. This usually prevented him from even trying to do his chores.

One thing that helped us was multitasking. "Wait!" I hear you say. "Doesn't multitasking split our attention between different tasks and ultimately make us less productive or negatively affect the quality of work we produce?" I thought the same thing! It turns out our brains have two systems—the automatic and the executive/cognitive. The automatic system guides 80%-90% of our activities every day and the executive system is needed for the remaining 10%-20%, where the effort needs to be intentional, purposeful and regulated. If you are driving a car, after a certain amount of time, driving becomes automatic. You don't think about shifting gears, pressing the gas or brake pedal. You do it all automatically. And while you are driving the car, you can also focus on the conversation you are having with your friend in the passenger seat. That conversation is utilizing the executive system. However, when you need to parallel park or there is an accident on the road ahead, you need to stop the conversation with your friend so your executive system can focus on this new task.

If Jack thinks that cleaning his room is boring, he will need to make use of his executive system in order to get it done. However, if we combine it with a task that is automatic but of interest to him, it can help him do the chores. So, while he was cleaning his room, he could be on the phone with his friend or listening to his favourite music to complete the task.

Jack doesn't like reading, especially when he perceives the text as long and boring. But keeping his sketchpad nearby and doodling and drawing while reading helps his executive system to be more focused on comprehending the content of the book or an article. And I would say that many non-ADHD people use these strategies regularly as well. I personally don't like cooking, but I have to do it every day. So, I combine it with a phone call to my parents, or enjoying my favourite movie or playlist.

Time

For bright and gifted ADHD children and adults, time can be a big problem. They don't know what time feels like or how much time they have left. Time blindness is kind of like being colour-blind, but with time. Just as someone who is colour-blind might struggle to differentiate between certain colours, someone with time blindness finds it tricky gauging the passing of time. They may feel like something took just a moment, when, in reality, it ate up half of their afternoon. Or they may think they still have a solid few hours to prepare for something, only to realize it is due in 15 minutes. And things that are *Not Now* do not need to be attended to. This means they find it difficult to prioritize what needs to be done first. Common issues include lacking a sense of urgency, constantly being late for appointments and underestimating how long a task will take.

They don't have an internal clock that perceives the passing of time, time is experienced from two types of time zones—*Now* and *Not Now*. This means if something is not happening *Now*, then it is happening *Not Now*.

They live in a permanent present, in the now. The *Not Now* is everything else—this enormous forever. The ADHD brain has a hard time both learning from previous mistakes and casting itself into the future to make plans. *Now* is all they focus on and they don't look into the future—there is lack of future thinking. Jack rarely learned from his previous mistakes and had difficulties answering questions about who he wanted to be when he grew up. When I tried to explain to him the consequences of his actions, he wasn't interested or worried about them in the slightest. He would say whatever he needed to in the moment to save himself or get what he wanted, even if it meant lying. This was an intense source of worry for me until I realised he genuinely couldn't comprehend that there would be repercussions for his actions. He lived every day in the moment, in the now, and didn't really know how time felt. Acting without thinking and not learning from past errors. Unable to complete projects on time, even though he had sufficient time to complete them. What an eye-opener it was to realise that, for him, these projects were just not that important as the deadline was in the future. It didn't matter if he was given weeks, months or years to work on the project, the due date was in the *Not Now,* and so wasn't important. It used to cause me so much stress because I am a planner to my core! I wanted him to break down the project into smaller chunks, assign timelines and complete part of it every day so it would be done well before the deadline.

It was very hard to accept that Jack thought differently. But I have to say, he works really well under pressure. The day before a due date when the project was in the *Now*, he would finally start to work on it and complete it on time. So, in this case, it was me who needed to learn a lesson from past experience. An assignment deadline needs to be close in time for Jack to feel any sense of urgency.

Experiencing Life More Intensely

The brain plays a crucial role in how we process our emotions. People with bright and gifted ADHD brains have the same emotions as everyone else. But what is different is the intensity of those emotions. Their emotions are not only more intense but can last longer and impact their lives and the lives of those around them to a greater degree. People with ADHD have a low emotional pain threshold.

The term intensity in this case relates to the strength of our reactions, and that strength equals the amount of pain we feel. As soon as I learned this, all the memories of Jack's tantrums and angry outbursts came rushing back. The reactions he had seemed out of proportion, but the strength of it represented the sheer volume of pain, anger and fear he felt in that moment and wasn't able to manage.

When we took away his phone as a punishment,

he would become enraged. His feelings would take over in the blink of an eye and his brain would enter flight, fight or freeze mode. In most cases, it chose fight mode—survival mode. This presented itself as an intense impulse to lash out and hit something or someone. And in those moments, he found himself unable to think about anything else, ruminating and circling back to the one thing he knew would make it stop. "Give me back my phone!" The emotions would gobble up all of the space in his head, consuming every thought like a computer virus devouring all of the space on a hard drive.

Emotional Outbursts & Impulsivity

Emotional regulation skills help us to process difficult experiences and feelings without spiralling out of control. Individuals with ADHD find it harder to regulate strong emotions such as anger. These emotions can completely take over. Especially if you add to this executive functioning challenges and the intensity of the emotions and experiences.

Thinking back to all the tantrums and meltdowns we went through, I can now from my observation notice the moments when Jack is getting triggered. Those are the moments when he feels pressured and feels frustrated—when he doesn't get what he wants and things are not going his way or when he feels threatened.

There can be only seconds between the trigger and him suddenly lashing out—like when a volcano erupts. The behaviour very often seemed like an overreaction, but because of the intensity of the feeling, he can get frustrated quickly and have trouble calming down. I learned my lesson... if you try to talk to him in this emotional state, it is like adding fuel to the fire. The situation can escalate quickly and we will be dealing not only with the emotional outburst, but on some occasions, with physical and verbal aggression. He is not able to manage his emotions, his reactions and his behaviour at that moment. This is called ADHD impulsivity. There is no reflection time—no pause between the impulse to act and the action.

Even those smallest moments can cause irritability and frustration. I was once standing behind the door of his bedroom, ready to knock and ask him to come down for dinner. Hesitating for a moment, I asked myself, "Do I really want to do it? What reaction can I expect?" I knocked. No response. "He must have his earphones in." I knocked again and then slowly opened the door.

I was met with, "What?! What do you want!? I am not hungry! Leave me alone!"

When he misinterprets what we are asking or the intent of our message, he can impulsively blurt out angry statements. As we don't use swear words in our house, I was surprised by how rich his swearing vocabulary is.

One minute, I am having a calm conversation with Jack, and the next minute, I feel like I am living with my own Incredible Hulk. You might be familiar with the movie where the calm and intelligent scientist transforms into a large green monster when he gets angry and frustrated.

I had to learn new strategies to deal with those situations. The most important thing is to manage my own emotions. As a parent, it is difficult to watch your child lose control over his emotions. I try to remember that he is not making the choice to act that way, to be so explosive. At the same time, I also need to keep my temper in check to avoid a screaming match. Otherwise, we have a situation where we are both in an escalated state and nothing good will come out of it. The best approach for me is to disengage when tensions run high. It is impossible to calm Jack down in his highly emotional state and I need to disengage and step away. I learned the hard way that it is better to walk away instead of trying to argue, negotiate, explain or get the last word in.

We will then revisit the situation at a later stage when things calm down.

When we reconvene, I try to help him normalize his emotions and help him recognize that we all have challenges with managing our emotions from time to time and that we all get angry and frustrated so he doesn't feel alone. I tell him stories about what helps me manage my emotions and that sometimes I fail to do so because nobody is perfect, but we all are humans.

Danger Zone – Do Not Tell!

Many of us don't like being told what to do. Giving orders or even making suggestions to a person with ADHD won't work and I learned from experience that it is often a huge mistake.

Being told what to do makes the ADHD brain feel confined and restricted. And, understandably, when people feel that way, they will often lash out and fight. We all, at some stage in our lives, have felt confined or trapped. Do you remember what that felt like? For me, it felt like there was no way out. It felt like the whole world was crashing down. I felt overwhelmed, a sense of hopelessness, despair, sadness, anger, frustration and fear.

Telling or even suggesting to Jack what he should do wasn't the best way to communicate with him. I needed to be more intentional and more thoughtful in how I approached him. And it turned out that the answer was actually asking him questions. I just needed to rephrase a suggestion or a command and pose it as a question. I needed to make him part of the decision-making process. And yes, it was hard to do. I felt like it took much longer and I felt like I was passing the control for the decisions and actions over to him, which is exactly what I was doing. And there were and will still be times when he makes the wrong decision. The main difference is that there won't be rage, tantrums, anger, yelling, screaming and our relationship will remain intact.

It was hard to accept it initially, but experimenting helped me see a huge difference.

One evening, I told him, "Please go and take a shower."

The response was, "No, I don't want to," and I repeated myself, justified my request by explaining that he hadn't taken a shower for three days and the importance of personal hygiene. And the response was, again, "No, I don't want to!" And I could see his emotions rising to the surface, I became more agitated and knew what was coming next, so I stopped and decided to give it another try the next day.

The following evening, I approached the situation with a question. "I have noticed that you haven't showered for the past four days, what are you planning to do about it?"

And he responded, "I will shower tomorrow morning."

So, I asked, "Would you like me to remind you to shower tomorrow morning?"

And to my surprise, he responded, "No, Mom, I will set a reminder on my phone."

Of course, it didn't always work out. But I knew that if he didn't want to take a shower, nothing would make him do it. Constant reminders would only agitate him, and shouting and arguing wouldn't change the outcome. It was very hard to accept that I wouldn't win every battle, but it was worth it to keep our relationship intact.

Brain vs. Mind – Distractibility

We all have what might be referred to as a network or system in our brain. There is a network that is activated when we are doing something physical or interacting with the world around us, be it working on a task or talking with someone. There is another network that is responsible for the mind wandering. The network responsible for mind wandering gets switched on when the network responsible for tasks is switched off. You can think of it as a light switch. If one is on, the other one is off. However, for people with bright and gifted ADHD brains, that switch doesn't work. The network responsible for mind wandering doesn't switch off. So, when they are trying to focus, the brain keeps telling them, "And what about this? And what about that? Let's focus on this new thing now." All of these distractions are continuously coming in.

When talking to Jack, I wanted him to pay attention to me because I had something to say that I really wanted him to hear. I would frequently say, "Look me in the eyes when I am talking to you," in the belief that if he was looking at me, he was paying attention to what I was saying. But if there was something else going on in the room or if there was a noise in the room distracting him, he wouldn't be able to focus on me. But this didn't mean that he wasn't trying to focus. This was also clearly visible in school. When teachers asked him to look at them or at the board but there were other things going on in the classroom, he would be unable to ignore the distraction.

Attention

Our brain produces 60,000 to 80,000 thoughts a day. Most of these thoughts are repetitious or negative. Unfortunately, nearly all human brains tend to focus on the negative. Our brains can filter out thoughts automatically based on what we have told ourselves is unimportant going by previous experiences. We can, therefore, think of attention as a highlighter. I remember when I was studying, I would read through a section of text in a book and highlight the important things, the keywords, the bits that stood out or seemed important to me. I would then focus specifically on those highlighted areas. Attention is critical in almost every area of life—school, work and in relationships. It allows you to focus on what is important to you and avoid distractions by filtering out what is not important.

Bright and gifted ADHD brains don't have those filters.

They don't have the highlighter that allows them to focus on what is important. For them, everything is equally important all the time. They split their attention between many things at once.

Because of that, people with ADHD can offer unique perspectives. These perspectives help them to see things that others wouldn't. When Jack has a problem and is interested in the outcome, he will find solutions we wouldn't even think of. Unfortunately, this creativity is often focused on avoiding rules or finding the loopholes in rules that don't suit him. "If I cannot have a PC today, I will go and buy an Xbox. That is not breaking rules." As I've mentioned before, in those moments as a parent, we were not sure if we were supposed to be upset with him or proud of his creativity!

Every strategy that we put in place for Jack stopped working after a couple of weeks. He would lose interest and get bored with them, and we would stop as soon as we noticed that they no longer worked. But instead, we should have done something to make it more interesting and more challenging. We should have focused on being more creative with those strategies, revisiting them and making them feel fresh and different. Another important lesson for us was observing him and noticing how long he remained interested in something. Having long conversations was always a challenge for us. He would lose interest after a few minutes, and when we kept going, he would get agitated and annoyed with us. So, we tracked how long a conversation with us would be of interest to him, especially how long he was able to focus fully and give us his undivided attention. Based on our observations, we would lose him after three or four minutes. When we had something important to communicate to him, we tried our best to make it as clear and concise as possible, aiming for the chat to not last longer than three minutes. He could do his homework for about 15 minutes—20 minutes at a stretch. So, we had to split homework into 15-minute chunks with breaks in between.

These strategies work most of the time, but there are still many occasions where doing something he considers boring is a challenge.

Fidgeting and Constant Movement

People used to believe that hyperactivity, constant movement and fidgeting interfered with the ability to concentrate. And so did I.

From the moment Jack was born, he was very active, restless, and unable to sit still. He always had to move or do something. As he got older, the need to move started manifesting itself differently. Hanging upside down from a chair or sofa, climbing on things, and trying to sit on tables and radiators. I would even go so far as to say he was 'bouncing off the walls'. This would get worse when he got bored, but there was still a need to move and fidget even when things were interesting to him. On many occasions when I wanted to talk to him, I would say, "Can you sit down?" Or, "Can you sit up and focus?" I truly believed that when he was constantly moving or handling something, he wasn't focusing and paying attention to what I was saying. That also came from the way I was brought up. Sitting still and looking people in their eyes when having a conversation was a sign you were paying attention to them. But with the bright and gifted ADHD brain, this is not the case. All that movement actually helps them focus and pay attention. That was a huge "Aha" moment for me. It turned what I knew and believed totally upside down. Now, we allow him to move, even though, for us, it is still very hard to talk and watch him as this goes against our beliefs. But I am sure that over time it will get easier to not only understand but to accept. Now we are thinking up some smaller activities that are not as visible as running around or hanging upside down—activities that he might be able to use at school to help him focus. Something that he can play with, possibly small fidget toys that wouldn't be distracting to others.

I have also learned that there are different types of hyperactivity, not just those associated with physical restlessness.

Every couple of months, Jack would need to change

up his room. He would ask for new pieces of furniture, then move everything around and redecorate. This is called drivenness. In adults, it manifests as the need and drive for the next thing. The urge to finish the current project and move on to what's next, such as changing jobs and moving houses.

Another type is cognitive or mental hyperactivity. The person's brain is going really fast, and they are constantly bombarded with thoughts and ideas and making connections that might not be relevant. I have noticed it multiple times talking with Jack—in the middle of a conversation or even in the middle of a sentence, he will change the topic to something completely different. He has suddenly made a new connection in his head that others don't see at all. I heard someone describing this type of hyperactivity as sitting in front of a TV with 100 channels. Someone else has the remote and keeps flipping between the channels and you don't have any control over the remote, so you are getting a little bit of one station and then a little bit of another. You are being bombarded with thoughts that you are not able to control.

"I forgot"

Our brain has a system or set of methods that it uses to temporarily hold and process new information alongside already stored information so we can apply it to a specific purpose. This is our working memory.

When we need to complete a task or solve a problem, we can tap into our memory and recall the information and resources we need. People with ADHD often experience deficits in working memory. Imagine you have to make a decision and you go to retrieve some past experiences, lessons learned, mistakes made, what worked and didn't work for you from your memory... however, when you reach into your mind, nothing is there. There are numerous challenges that people experience due to a working memory deficit.

In Jack's case, I have seen poor follow-through. He commits to things with the best of intentions, but then doesn't get them done.

On multiple occasions after we had a full conversation about something, he would claim to not remember what we discussed.

Working memory is like computer storage—a system to store, manage and retrieve information. But like computer storage, working memory has a limit to how much information it can hold. After observing Jack (who was 14 at this point), we estimated that he could hold about three pieces of information. So, if I asked him to go upstairs and complete five tasks, he would come back and have done only half of them. When I asked, "What about the remaining tasks?" he wouldn't remember them at all. Now I pick at most three tasks and ask him to just focus on those. Writing things down and making it part of a routine has also been a huge help for us. Even now, when I ask him to do something, he asks me, "Can you please write it down for me on a sticky note?" At some stage, we are hoping that he will start writing those notes and reminders for himself.

Working memory is also related to sequencing—the order in which we do things.

Jack always had challenges with comprehension. Reading was something he found boring, and when he read or listened to something, he was able to recall the details but not the order in which they occurred. He also was able to remember small details but couldn't remember some of the key events. We started using mind maps, which allowed him to note down everything he could recall and then elaborate on each point. We still play a lot of working memory games at weekends or during car rides to help him improve his working memory with practice.

Struggle with Hygiene

We all have to make transitions throughout the day, from one activity to another. Children transition from home to school, from class to class, from playtime to sleep time. For many of us, transitioning from one task to another is pretty natural and we don't have to think about it. But those with bright and gifted ADHD brains have to think about the what, the when, and the how.

Their brains want to continue doing whatever it is they are currently engaged in, and moving from one task to another may feel uncomfortable or even boring. They lack the executive control needed to transition from one thing to the next.

For Jack, getting in the shower represents a ton of work. But once he is in there, he could be there for an hour. I always wondered why it is so difficult for him to get in if he is enjoying it so much that he doesn't want to get out! But I never thought about the fact that getting out of the shower could also be a struggle. I never considered pausing to think about how many steps are involved in the process of taking a shower. He has to undress, get in the shower, turn on the water, put shampoo and soap on, rinse it off, turn off the water, get out of the shower, dry himself and get dressed again. For him, thinking of all these tasks is really challenging.

Brushing teeth is another example. After constant reminders, he would eventually go into the bathroom, spend 30 seconds there and come out. "Did you brush your teeth?" I asked.

"No, I forgot," he would say and head back in. I couldn't believe that he could enter the bathroom with one purpose and still forget. But by the time he had reached the bathroom and closed the door, he had genuinely forgotten to brush his teeth.

To address this, we decided to create a proper routine.

Brushing teeth is now the first thing that happens in the morning and he has visual reminders in the bathroom to give him a hint of what he is supposed to be doing there. During weekends, we all brush our teeth together. We agreed that certain days would be shower days in the same way that, in our house, Saturdays are cleaning days and Sundays are family days, so he now has shower days. We also started combining it with activities he truly enjoys, such as listening to music or watching a video. Sometimes he succeeds and sometimes he doesn't. Ideally, we would want him to take showers every day, but taking into consideration the challenges he is facing, I feel every little step forward is a reason to celebrate.

Messiness, is it Laziness?

Some people are naturally neat and organized, while others seem to exist in a state of constant clutter.

Many individuals with ADHD can be messy most of the time. If you need a real-life example, just come and look at Jack's room! You will find clean and dirty clothes in mixed heaps on the floor or shoved into the wardrobe because I asked him to tidy up his room. Among the heaps of clothes, you will find empty sweet packets, and documents (usually from the school for us to sign) hanging out of his overflowing backpack, or torn in shreds on the floor.

He not only makes a mess, but once the mess is made, he just walks away from it. I've lost count of the times I've reminded him to not leave the top off his toothpaste or to flush the toilet.

I used to make a big deal out of it. When he was smaller, he did all the chores with me and enjoyed them. It was important to him to keep his room tidy. Here is a funny story. We taught Jack how to pee sitting down on the toilet rather than standing. He understood why when he saw that the toilet needed to be cleaned. He was only about five when one of his friends came over for a sleepover. His friend went to the bathroom and Jack followed him. Then I heard yelling, "Can't you sit down while you pee? Who do you think will be cleaning the toilet after you?!" That was how important cleanliness was to him. Therefore, I have to admit that I assumed all this messiness was just a result of Jack's laziness or carelessness.

Now I understand that there is an underlying cause, which explains why he has trouble with the skills needed to clean up and stay organized—his executive functioning skills. Now I can approach this situation with empathy. An adult friend of mine who also has this amazing ADHD brain explained to me how Jack may feel when told to tidy his room. "Imagine, you have never seen a Rubik's Cube before and you have very little experience with puzzles. I ask you to complete the Rubik's Cube but without asking for help. Oh, and you have only 30 minutes to solve it! Where would you even start?" Sounds like an impossible task—a task you cannot really conquer, one with no clear beginning or end.

On many occasions, I have asked Jack to clean his room, and he has headed upstairs to clean. Then I hear, "Mom, it is done! Come and check!" And when I went upstairs, it looked like he hadn't even started it. When I asked him about it, he said, "Yes, I cleaned the room, I picked up my socks, and I dusted." His interpretation of 'clean your room' was very different to mine and, of course, that did not produce the result I was expecting.

Instead of asking him to clean his room, I now break it down into small tasks and put those tasks into writing:

- Move clothes from the floor to the laundry basket.
- Bring the laundry basket down to the laundry room.
- Collect all the trash from your room and put it in the bin.
- Bring the bin down and take the trash outside.

You get the idea. These step-by-step instructions and visual prompts help him to remember what specifically needs to be accomplished.

In addition, we combine tasks that have a heavier executive function 'load' with tasks that are automated and enjoyable... like listening to his favourite music. We also estimate the time each task will take so he knows that he will only be tidying for the next 10 or 15 minutes. We have also found that a timer is helpful so he knows when he began and how long it takes for him to finish tasks.

To make things simpler for him, instead of asking him to keep all his clean and ironed clothes in the wardrobe, we have bought open baskets with different colours. The green basket is for clean and ironed clothes, the blue basket is for school clothes and the red basket is for dirty clothes. This means he doesn't have to put his clothes away in the wardrobe, he can still throw them, but instead of throwing them on the floor, he throws them into a basket, keeping the clean and dirty clothes separated.

What You Focus On Grows

As mentioned before, our brain generates 60,000 to 80,000 thoughts a day and most of them are negative. Unfortunately, these negative thoughts are treated as though they are real, when, actually, they are just random negative thoughts generated automatically by our brain. Our automatic brain is fast and strong.

Thankfully, we don't only have our brain, we also have our unique mind.

The mind is like a general in the command centre. This general can pause and make thoughtful decisions. It can make decisions on what thoughts we focus our attention on and help us override the automatic behaviour of our brain.

Ideally, we want our brain and mind to work together in harmony.

Unlocking My Child's Superpowers

ADHD – 'Attention Deficit Hyperactivity Disorder'

It seems so odd to call a condition a disorder when this condition comes with so many strengths and positive features. In the beginning, I only focused on the negative, on the 'red flags', on the things Jack struggled with. But now that I better understand how his amazing ADHD brain works and accept that his behaviour is not who he is, I have started noticing what he is doing well—his 'superpowers'.

Resilience & Perseverance

Every day, he encounters a new struggle, and on many occasions, has to work harder than his peers to overcome it. But he never gives up and instead has become more determined to achieve his goals. He possesses boundless energy and remarkable endurance.

Flexibility

His mind can quickly shift from one thing to another, and this gives him tremendous flexibility and adaptability.

Problem-Solving

He has an outstanding ability to think outside of the box and come up with unique solutions that others haven't even considered.

Divergent Thinking

He is able to think of innovative ways to overcome knowledge constraints, and brainstorm and generate a range of alternative and unique solutions. He can harness his creativity in a strange and wonderful way.

Unlimited Energy

He has plenty of energy to dominate in sports, tackle any tasks at hand and being so energetic makes him fun to be around.

Excel and Rock Things He Is Passionate About

He is willing to dedicate endless amounts of time and energy to work on perfecting something that he is really interested in and passionate about.

Willingness to Take Risks

Yes, sometimes he doesn't think things through, but often, this helps him get ahead as he is willing to take risks and get out of his comfort zone.

Awesome Imagination

He can use his imagination to create incredible stories and I have no doubt that he will be able to dream up new inventions. The sky is the limit for him!

Curiosity

He has an endless curiosity for new things. He appreciates new ideas and concepts. While others are focusing on a single topic or problem, he can see and perceive parts of the overall picture that are often not appreciated by others.

Charisma

His infectious smile says a million words. He is passionate and enthusiastic, and people want to be around him. He constantly reminds me that perfection is uninteresting.

Impulsivity and Spontaneity

Yes, I wrote 'impulsivity'. Looking at it from my new vantage point, I can see that he trusts his own instincts, which helps him turn his dreams into realities, make quick decisions and seize opportunities.

Vision

He sees the world through a completely different lens. He is often able to put a different perspective on a situation or a problem.

Unconventional Education

The end of summer marked the beginning of a new school year, which filled us with a sense of dread. Jack's aversion to school was deeply rooted, and we feared the battles that lay ahead. Would he refuse to go to school again? The question lingered ominously. The first two days of school, however, held a glimmer of hope. Jack begrudgingly attended, perhaps buoyed by the anticipation of seeing friends. But, on the third day, the dream came crashing down. Jack claimed to be sick, and we, hesitant but understanding, decided to keep him home. Days turned into a couple of weeks, and a pattern emerged again. The refusal to go to school became a stubborn routine, and our efforts to reason with him yielded little success. We reached out to the school's principal for assistance, who, in turn, engaged the Educational Welfare officer. Her call the next day marked a turning point. As we shared our struggles and fears, she gently proposed an idea: home-schooling. We decided to take the leap and applied for home education. With the decision made, I assumed the role of Jack's teacher, applying all the lessons I had learned, not only in a home but also 'school' environment. Each evening, I meticulously planned the subjects we would tackle the next day. It had been a while since I attended school myself, so I needed to re-learn many concepts. This newfound responsibility also demanded a major change in my daily routine as I still had a regular job that I just couldn't set aside. To be honest, it was a balancing act, but one I willingly embraced for the sake of our family and Jack's future. Our daily routine was structured and predictable. Instead of the traditional 9 AM start time, we began our day at 11 AM, allowing Jack time to wake up and start the day with things he enjoyed. We discovered that Jack's focus lasted about 20 minutes at a stretch, so we worked with his attention span rather than against it. Regular breaks, movement, and fidgeting were not only allowed but encouraged. One surprising addition to our home classroom was a treadmill. For subjects that required memorization, Jack stepped onto the treadmill as I taught him. To my amazement, he focused better and retained information more effectively while in motion.

A whiteboard became our canvas for visualizing complex ideas, and I learned how to simplify topics, explaining them in a way that a child could grasp. Big words were replaced with clear, understandable language, eliminating an unnecessary barrier to his learning. Our lessons became fun and interactive. We talked, walked, and even added humour into the mix. Sometimes, I would throw in a bit of theatrical flair, re-enacting topics to make them memorable! Irish, a subject neither Tom nor I were well-versed in, required additional support. The school was able to arrange for an Irish teacher to visit every Friday. Math proved to be another challenge, but finding a tutor who could accommodate Jack's schedule proved difficult. That's when I had an epiphany—if the tutor couldn't teach Jack in the evenings, they could teach me instead. Thus, I became both a student and a teacher of mathematics, ensuring Jack received the guidance he needed. As we were getting the hang of home-schooling, we faced another hurdle. Jack's application that we submitted months and months ago with Child Mental Health Services had been rejected due to the perceived mildness of his symptoms. The decision left us baffled and frustrated. What would be considered 'severe' enough? We turned to our family doctor for support and he shared our concerns. He resubmitted the application, and we have resigned ourselves to another long wait, still hopeful that Jack will receive the assistance he needs and deserves. In the midst of these challenges, our commitment to supporting Jack remains unwavering. We are embracing homeschooling as a path of empowerment and discovery, adapting our lives to nurture his growth. It's a journey filled with uncertainties, but one thing is certain... we will face it together as a family.

Making the World Work For Your Child

Since you are reading this book, I assume you are a parent.

You might be wondering and questioning what to do to gain control over your child, but you know that no amount of yelling, arguing or punishment will work.

Your friends, family, and maybe even your partner may insist that if you were just a bit stricter, if you just stopped accepting this behaviour and those tantrums, things would be different.

But they don't experience your day-to-day reality and, even if they try to understand, they will never know what it is like to live through those moments of helplessness and pain. Their children may also misbehave, but their brains are wired differently. Their children can be reasoned with, yours cannot.

Know and always remember one thing. Your child's behaviour isn't because of your parenting. It is not because you sent them to playschool too early or because you stayed at home with them and gave them your undivided attention. It is not because of the arguments you had with your partner about parenting strategies. It is not because of that one thing you did or didn't do when they were little. It is not because you lost your patience or were too patient with them.

Their behaviour is not because you don't love them enough or you don't love them in the right way, and it is not because you didn't discipline them hard enough. It is just the way they are and how their brain is wired.

You are not a terrible parent. Nothing you did caused it. It is not your fault and it is not their fault for that matter.

Parenting has rarely been easy for anyone, and parenting a child with ADHD can be even harder. But I do hope and believe that it will get easier if we just understand the way their brain works, the way they think, the way they process emotions and we give ourselves permission to make the world work for them. In a world that often moulds us to follow predefined paths, from the way we learn to how we think and operate, it is crucial to pause and question it. What we learned from our parents and what we practiced ourselves can serve as guiding lights, but they aren't the only way of accomplishing things. Embracing my child's uniqueness made me consider another, more authentic path that resonates with his strengths in a world that can be tailored to fit him just as much as he fits into it. I truly believe that being a parent requires being a protector, soundboard, problem-solver, mentor, teacher, coach, sometimes a detective, but most importantly, being your child's biggest cheerleader.

Now that I know more about ADHD, I am also aware and accepting of the fact that he may need our support longer than others, that he will (and will need to) challenge the status quo and accomplish things in his own time and in his own way.

While I acknowledge the inherent uncertainty of the future, I firmly believe that there is no one-size-fits-all approach to education and the pursuit of dreams. Jack will chart his own unique path and discover the methods and strategies that resonate most with his passions and that work best for him, ultimately leading him to a future filled with purpose, growth and fulfilment. As a mother, what more could I want for my child? Yes, he is not doing things the way we had hoped, imagined or been taught, but he is doing them his way.

My mission is now clear. True parenting isn't about shaping our children to fit the mould. It is about nurturing their individuality and helping them become the best version of themselves, empowering them to embrace their true selves and supporting them while they fearlessly chart their unique paths in life. I am determined to support other families who are on a similar journey. Together, we can nurture the extraordinary potential that lies within each child, embracing their differences and celebrating their individuality.

Printed in Great Britain
by Amazon